FERRARI

FORMULA 1 RACING TEAM

FERRARI

FORMULA 1 RACING TEAM

DAVID TREMAYNE
SECOND EDITION

Haynes Publishing

DEDICATION

For Chris Amon and Ignazio Giunti, the two Ferrari drivers who excited me most, and for whom Fate dealt the wrong cards. And for Count Wolfgang von Trips, whom Fate similarly cheated.

First published in November 1998
Second edition published in April 2001
Reprinted in December 2001

A catalogue record for this book is available from the British Library

ISBN 1 85960 830 2

Library of Congress catalog card no. 00-136550

Haynes North America Inc.,
861 Lawrence Drive, Newbury Park,
California 91320, USA.

Published by Haynes Publishing, Sparkford,
Nr Yeovil, Somerset BA22 7JJ, UK.

Tel. 01963 442030 Fax 01963 440001
Int. tel. +44 1963 442030 Fax +44 1963 440001
E-mail: sales@haynes-manuals.co.uk
Web site: www.haynes.co.uk

Designed and typeset by G&M, Raunds, Northamptonshire
Printed and bound in Great Britain by J. H. Haynes & Co. Ltd

All photographs are by Formula One Pictures unless credited otherwise in the caption.

Contents

Acknowledgements   6

Introduction   7

Chapter 1:   The prancing horse stumbles   13

Chapter 2:   Politics and passion   32

Chapter 3:   Great expectations   56

Chapter 4:   Getting the mix right   81

Chapter 5:   Full gallop   106

Chapter 6:   Qualified success   136

Chapter 7:   Double top   160

Appendix 1:   Ferrari – race results   181

Appendix 2:   Ferrari – team statistics   189

Appendix 3:   Ferrari – most successful drivers   190

Acknowledgements

ountless people have helped with the writing of this book, giving their time and their views with generous spirit. I'd like to thank: Michele Alboreto; Jean Alesi; John Barnard; Rubens Barrichello; Gerhard Berger; Claudio Berro; Ross Brawn; Ivan Capelli; Ron Dennis; Oreste Giovannini; Antonio Ghini; Phil Hill; Ed Irvine; Eddie Irvine; Kathleen Irvine; Sonia Irvine; Nicola Larini; Niki Lauda; Nigel Mansell; Luca di Montezemolo; Dr Harvey Postlethwaite; Alain Prost; Attilio Ruffo; Michael Schumacher; Nigel Stepney; Jean Todt; Tim Watson; Nigel Wollheim and Brock Yates. Thanks also to David Hayhoe, author of the *Grand Prix Data Book*, for supplying the statistics contained in the Appendices.

Introduction

In 1929, Enzo Ferrari 'borrowed' the Prancing Horse logo used by Italian First World War aircraft fighter ace Francesco Baracca, and then mounted it upon the yellow shield of Modena. In doing so he created a race team that would become a legend, a team that, despite his death in August 1988, would endure and prosper.

Ferrari is Formula One. Many seriously doubt that the sport's credibility could survive if the team were ever to withdraw from competition. An aura has grown around it, based partly on its glorious history, and partly on its idiosyncratic ways of doing things. Ferrari is different. It is the only team that has always manufactured its engines as well as the chassis. It is also the only team which has raced in F1 right from the inception of the World Championship in 1950. It is therefore the thread that binds together the disparate generations the sport has spawned.

In Italy, Ferrari is not just a Grand Prix motor racing team. It is to its followers what Manchester United and the England team, rolled into one, might be to football fanatics this side of the Channel. Yet it is even more than that. The constant pressure compares with every nightmare that England football boss Glenn Hoddle endured during the 1998 World Cup, multiplied by a factor of at least ten, because Ferrari is not just every Italian male's interest, it is his ego and his manhood. A blow against Ferrari is a blow against the national psyche.

Ferrari is a religion. A religion pursued with all the fervour of zealotry. There is a story that graphically illustrates the heights to which passions may be inflamed when Formula One engines run in Italy. Two fans, 'tifosi', as they are known, sat together in the grandstand at Monza, watching the Italian Grand Prix in 1966. One had eyes only for the scarlet Ferrari of a 32-year-old aristocrat named Ludovico Scarfiotti, scion of the Agnelli family which owns Fiat and which, three years hence, would own a large share of Ferrari. The other rooted for Englishman John Surtees, the feisty 32-year-old former motorcycle racer who, in winning the World Championship with Ferrari in 1964, had become the only man ever to take world titles on two and four wheels, but who had earlier that season turned his back on the great Italian team's politics after a furious row with them. Manager Eugenio Dragoni favoured Surtees's Italian team-mate Lorenzo Bandini and put around the suggestion that the Englishman had never fully recovered from a serious accident in Canada in 1965. Surtees, ever his own man, was not standing for that and had left to drive for the British Cooper team. Worse still, from the Scarfiotti fan's point of view, Surtees's bulky green car was powered by a V12 engine from Ferrari's across-town rival, Maserati.

Scarfiotti's supporter remained seated. A knife protruded from his chest

---

During the race an argument which became ever more heated developed between the two fans, but when the crowd trooped from the autodromo, the majority ecstatic at Scarfiotti's home victory, his supporter remained seated, forever deaf to the adulatory screams. A knife protruded from his chest.

Motor racing is a national obsession in Italy, home for the Grand Prix at Monza every September. And feelings for Ferrari run high among the spectators. Hearts and emotion are worn on the fans' sleeves with an endearing passion unclouded by self-consciousness. It has sired that breed of superfan known collectively as the tifosi. It is perhaps apposite that the word tifosi derives from typhoid, *il tifo*, since ecstatic fans are said to display similar symptoms to one in the throes of typhoid.

Italy's tifosi are arguably the best informed fans of them all. They adore Ferrari, and they always seem to find a way to see the action. Those who do not camp out on the hills within the Imola circuit, home of the San Marino Grand Prix each May, get by with special little wooden seats that look like swings stolen from the local park, except that the chains have hooks on the ends so that they can be slung over the top of Imola's concrete walls to provide an excellent view, until the occupants get moved on. When this happens, it is merely a case of relocating somewhere else along the walls. Many of the tifosi have their hair cropped, with only a Prancing Horse standing out, while Italy's national colours or Ferrari's black on yellow livery complete the effect.

At Monza the same fans have equally ingenious methods of getting the best view. Once, one got into the paddock by the simple expedient of wearing a uniform and bringing his dog, muzzled and on a leash just like those of the officials. He was only rumbled when the dog failed to emulate the unpleasant mien of the real thing.

There are pockets of tifosi all around the world, cheering on Michael Schumacher and Rubens Barrichello as they race for Scuderia Ferrari Marlboro. When Ferraris break down the tifosi scream and rant. When they win, the tifosi wins too. For them a Ferrari victory is as close as they can get to heaven on Earth, and whenever this joyous moment occurs the church bells ring all round Modena and Maranello.

But what lies behind the countless inspirations for such unquestioning adoration of Ferrari?

Enzo Ferrari was born in Modena on 18 February 1898. In 1929, in Viale Trento Trieste in the small Italian village of his birth, he created the Scuderia Ferrari, a racing team which would enter its members in motor races. By 1938 his team's successes, mainly with Alfa Romeo machinery, had elevated him to the position of racing manager with the Milanese company. Two years later however came a bitter divorce, and the foundation of Auto Avio Costruzioni Ferrari, in the old Scuderia Ferrari headquarters. Its primary purpose was to manufacture machine tools, principally oleodynamic grinding machines. Under the terms of his divorce, Ferrari was not supposed to put his name to

Competitive racing takes good pitwork, and the Ferrari mechanics continued to uphold the reputation of their predecessors by servicing Schumacher and Irvine in impressive style.

the manufacture of racing cars for the next four years, but as early as 1940 his company began to study and design an eight-cylinder 1.5-litre car which would come to be known as the 815. Two of these competed in that year's Mille Miglia. Three years later, after the Second World War had interrupted his plans, Ferrari moved his company from Modena to Maranello, continuing with the machine tool manufacture for another year. With the cessation of hostilities came a change of company name, simply to Ferrari. And with that came the 125 Sport, a 1.5-litre car with a V12 engine, the car that started a legend.

Throughout his life Enzo Ferrari assiduously cultivated his mystique

---

Since the inception of the World Championship, and up until the end of the 2000 season, Ferrari had won a record 135 Grand Prix victories (five more than McLaren). Its cars had taken pole position 137 times (27 more than McLaren). They had set fastest lap on 144 occasions (34 more than Williams). And in a record 636 Grand Prix participations they had scored 2,528.5 World Championship points (43 more than McLaren).

Eight men have now won World Championship crowns in Ferraris: Alberto Ascari (1952 and '53); Juan Manuel Fangio (1956); Mike Hawthorn (1958); Phil Hill (1961); John Surtees (1964); Niki Lauda (1975 and '77), Jody Scheckter (1979) and, most recently, Michael Schumacher in 2000. The team has won the World Championship for Constructors in 1961, 1964, 1975, 1976, 1977, 1979, 1982 and 1983, 1999 and again in 2000. No other team can match that score.

Ferrari was hardly less successful in the World Sportscar Championship, as a one-time record of nine victories at Le Mans testifies. Eight victories in the gruelling pan-Italian Mille Miglia, and seven in the Targa Florio in Sicily, merely add lustre to an already glittering heritage.

Throughout his life, Enzo Ferrari assiduously cultivated his mystique, declaring that today's cars held no interest for him. All that mattered were tomorrow's. Once his machines had done their work, they were left to moulder in the back lot at Maranello, discarded like old soldiers laid to rest.

He scarcely took any greater interest in his drivers. To him they were honoured to be given the chance of driving his creations, and more than any other manufacturer in a sporting history that has seen its share of dispassionate men, he regarded them as expendable.

The roll call of those who paid the highest price for the honour of serving Ferrari is chilling: Eugenio Castellotti; Marquis Alfonso de Portago; Luigi Musso; Peter Collins; Count Wolfgang von Trips; Lorenzo Bandini; Ignazio Giunti and Gilles Villenueve; all succumbed for the cause. Castellotti's death was a cruel illustration of how enslaved they all were to the legend of

Ferrari. He had been enjoying a holiday in March 1957 with his Italian actress lover, Delia Scala, but was hastily summoned to the Modena track on Ferrari's specific order, to defend the team's lap record against attack from arch-rival Maserati. The so-called record was meaningless, but Castellotti knew better than to disobey Ferrari's order. Angry but acquiescent, he drove back to Modena and rode into history on the back of a fatal driving error. Ferrari, typically, sought to console Scala, as he would not long afterwards, with Musso's mistress.

Ferrari loved to heap pressure upon his drivers as he pitted one against the other in the belief that internal friction was the father of great performances. He could be Machiavellian, and liked to do this ruthlessly and mercilessly. He was cruelly dismissive of those he perceived to be weak, and liked to treat the men who risked their lives for him as if they were his personal marionettes. His reasons were simple: his beloved red cars were really all that mattered. Maranello was thus always a hotbed of polemics, and remained so for many years even after his death. It was as if it had become a way of life that nobody knew how to shake off.

The autocracy, allied to the glamour of the good times and the angst of the bad, forged and tempered the team,

With just hours to go before the deciding round of the '98 World Championship, Schumacher passes by Hakkinen's McLaren, with his new helmet in hand.

The team, the car. The elegant F2001 would win first time out in Melbourne.

creating a unique charisma as fortune ebbed and flowed. Like any team Ferrari has its flaws, but no other has so totally come to embody the world over the pride and passion, the romance and spirit, that is Grand Prix motor racing.

Some legendary teams failed to survive long without the men who founded them and provided the driving force, but Ferrari remains an organisation in which no individual is greater than the sum of its parts. It has a mystique and charm all its own. It was totally apposite as the World Championship celebrated its 50th anniversary in 2000 that Ferrari should finally win not just another Constructors' World Championship, but the all-important Drivers' title too.

David Tremayne
Harrow and Stapleton, 2001

Chapter *1*

The prancing
horse stumbles

The first elements of Ferrari's success in the 2000 World Championships were drawn together in 1992 as Luca di Montezemolo, the mastermind of Niki Lauda's domination in the mid-1970s, returned to take control. The 1991 season had been a disaster, following Alain Prost's near miss in 1990, but 1992 was to be even worse. This was

John Barnard's elegant 412T evoked echoes of the 1961 'Sharknose' in the initial shape of its side radiator intake ducts. Di Montezemolo, Alesi, Berger, Todt and Larini (in the cockpit) unveiled the car to an enthusiastic media at Fiorano in February 1994.

not just because of the dearth of results but because it also proved conclusively that the previous season's slump from the highly competitive pitch had not been an unpleasant fluke.

Despite his credentials, di Montezemolo faced a Herculean task in resuscitating the failing horse, and as 1992 moved into 1993 it became brutally apparent just how much of a mountain the team faced, as Williams and Renault continued to redefine the parameters of F1 performance, continually moving the goalposts and leaving McLaren and Ferrari floundering in their wake. And the more the appallingly uncompetitive performances continued, the more frequently was the view aired that perhaps, after its glorious decades of competition, Ferrari really couldn't hack it after all. They put old horses out to grass, and some expressed the almost heretical view that it might be better to do the same with Ferrari's once-prancing stallion rather than watch it stumble pathetically and fall at so many hurdles.

Lauda, who together with di Montezemolo, had been so instrumental in forging that Seventies success, returned in 1992 at Luca's behest as a consultant. Here is an example of the pragmatic Austrian's sense of humour, and refusal to dress anything up. Marlboro produces an annual pocket-book which contains the results and facts and figures of every Grand Prix since the World Championship was inaugurated in 1950. Although his individual statistics mention the 1976 German GP, the race result itself, else-

Even when the results are rather flat, the glamour of a team like Ferrari is never far away.

Before long the sculpted ducts had disappeared, but the 412T was nevertheless a quantum leap over its predecessors. It had arguably the most powerful engine of them all, and superbly forgiving handling, but its thirsty V12 proved a continuing drawback.

where in the book, makes no mention of him. Because the fiery accident which befell him came in the first part of the race, which was then subsequently restarted as a new race altogether, he is not officially credited with starting the event that nearly killed him. This was once mentioned to him, at which point he gave a deep laugh and in his clipped deadpan manner demanded to know: 'What happened to my ear then?'

Lauda's insistence on telling things the way they are was a godsend to Ferrari during this troubled period in the early 1990s. By no stretch of the imagination was he ever a yes-man, and he could be relied upon to act as a

perfect sounding board for di Montezemolo. Of course, the critics immediately pounced upon Luca for, as they saw it, harking back to the old days by resurrecting Lauda and team manager Sante Ghedini, but he knew that he had to establish datums rapidly, and that he needed people he could trust. As usual, Lauda shot from the hip.

'Ferrari didn't work,' he said quickly in his clipped tones. 'That's my opinion. Then in came Montezemolo. And with him there was an opportunity there for me which wasn't there before.

'I'm here purely to advise. I'm here to use my experience to Ferrari's benefit. I have to watch, to stand and observe. But then I will ask, "Why do it that way? Let's try this way."

'My job is not to drive or tell the drivers how to do that. Not at all. What the driver has always needed to do most is to communicate to his engineers what the car is doing. That's the key. My job is to be the interpreter, the man who pulls together the things that Luca does, and Harvey Postlethwaite, Jean-Claude Migeot, Claudio Lombardi and Sante Ghedini.'

It's a matter of getting the right people into the right jobs

---

It was an independent role, and remained so for some time, and for Lauda it was the perfect antidote to his full-time occupation of running his airline, LaudaAir. By the time that ran into trouble at the turn of the century, however, Lauda was no longer part of the new Ferrari. But back then he insisted right from the start that any attempt to compare Ferrari in 1977, and Ferrari in 1992, would be invidious. 'You can't even really compare last year with this,' he said. 'There's been a complete change of management, a new way to go. It's a matter of getting the right people into the right jobs, but to get the results it takes time. Because we inherited a car from last year's people, we have to modify it and make sure that it's going to work, which is a difficult job.'

What made it more difficult still was that 1992 was the year of Nigel Mansell and the actively suspended Williams-Renault FW14. In retrospect, nobody else had a chance, let alone a team still trying to make sense from former chaos.

'What I'm saying is that the result of these people, you won't see really before the same time next year,' Lauda counselled. But he would be wrong. Circumstances would dictate that it would be an awful lot longer than that. The F92A was such a fundamentally complex car, with its unusual twin-floor aerodynamics, that the French magazine *Auto Hebdo* depicted Alesi in a cartoon pushing his red 'locomotive' around Interlagos ahead of Martin Brundle's Benetton, using the gap between the two floors as a handy place in which to store his firewood. But the reality was not a matter for laughter. In a dispiriting season, Alesi's best results were third places in Spain and Canada, and fourths in Brazil and Australia. He crashed in four other races. Poor Ivan Capelli fared even worse, taking fifth in Brazil and sixth in Hungary, and crashing six times. By the end of the season his F1 career was all but dead.

Nor was 1993 any better, as Gerhard Berger came bouncing back into the fold in John Barnard's interim F93A. There wasn't much wrong with Barnard's engineering ability, but the execution of the car's active suspension gave both Berger and Alesi some

At last the faithful Berger could sense serious progress, and got off to a good start to the season with a series of podium finishes.

frights. By far the most dangerous and embarrassing was when the suspension malfunctioned as Berger accelerated down the pit road to rejoin the Portuguese GP at Estoril. The car wrenched itself from his control and promptly turned sharp left across the main straight, down which JJ Lehto's Sauber and Derek Warwick's Footwork were speeding on the wrong side of 180mph (290kph). By sheer miracle neither struck the broadside Ferrari before it crashed heavily into the barrier opposite the pits, leaving Berger to limp home on foot and counting his good fortune. A catastrophic tragedy had only narrowly been averted, and the Italian media had the sort of field day frenzied sharks dream of.

By sheer miracle neither struck the Ferrari before it crashed

---

Second place for Alesi at Monza and third at Monaco, allied to third for Berger in Hungary and fourth in Canada looked pretty feeble as Prost and Hill dominated the season.

What Ferrari most needed, Lauda insisted, was patience. 'Luca is there, which is a guy who is not going to change his ways through pressure from the media. Who knows what he is doing. He is the guarantee that nothing will happen like that.

'Ferrari's biggest problem is its past,' he said, but his belief remained intact that the great team could rise again to challenge Williams, McLaren and the increasingly competitive Benetton, for whom Michael Schumacher had been performing with more and more promise. The Portuguese race in which Berger had crashed so spectacularly had marked the young German's second Grand Prix triumph.

'It needs time, that's all I can say,' Lauda repeated. 'You can't do it overnight.' But it would take so long that Ferrari would begin to feel as if daylight had been suspended altogether.

Behind the scenes, Ferrari was believed to be strongly behind the FIA's plan to ban many of the electronic systems that were threatening to usurp the role of the drivers, and active suspension featured high on the list for the axe. After much argument, the FIA got its way, and Ferrari faced 1994 buoyed with fresh hope. John Barnard's 412 was an outstandingly elegant car that held great promise, but again it was a relatively disappointing year as Benetton and Williams slogged it out against the tragic backcloth of the deaths of Roland Ratzenberger and Ayrton Senna at Imola. But there were moments of brightness. At Hockenheim, Berger breathed new life into Scuderia Ferrari when he secured the team's first victory since Alain Prost had claimed the Spanish Grand Prix in September 1990. Thus ended Ferrari's longest spell without a win. And that success could well have been repeated shortly afterwards by Alesi at

Alesi, however, missed early races after straining his neck in a heavy shunt during testing at Mugello.

Passion, and a way of life

For drivers the chequered flag usually signals the end of a Grand Prix; but for other supporting members of Scuderia Ferrari Marlboro it triggers another, very different kind of contest of distance versus time. For the moment the flag drops, the team's personnel engage in a frantic rush to break camp, pack up the cars in their transporters, and head back to base to prepare for the next venue.

It's a very demanding scenario. Up to 17 races, packed into a schedule that begins in Australia in March and ends in Japan in November, and usually runs on an every-other-week basis. As Formula One makes its way around the globe, the sheer logistical demands present a fearsome challenge to those whose job it is to keep up.

For seven years Oreste Giovannini has been a 'truckie', a member of an elite band whose job it is not just to drive the cars around the world in their colourful transporters, but to set up the team's supporting infrastructure at the races. There is close to 100 tons of this.

Giovannini leaves Scuderia Ferrari Marlboro's base in Maranello at 6 o'clock in the morning on the Monday prior to a race, and usually arrives with his transporter at the circuit by Tuesday evening. There, he will wash down the truck to preserve Scuderia Ferrari Marlboro's high standards of professionalism, then park it precisely in the space allocated by the organisers in the paddock. FIA officials are very fussy about all the trucks being parked parallel with white lines, equidistant from their fellows and perfectly in line with them. It is one of Bernie Ecclestone's orders that a professional front should be presented at all times.

'On Wednesday morning we unload and set everything up in the pit garage,' Giovannini explains, 'so that by Thursday morning, when the race team mechanics arrive, everything is ready.'

The truck drivers also have other roles to fulfil at the races. 'It is also my responsibility to ensure that the race team has all the spare parts that it needs,' Giovannini says. 'Each time we get back to base I must prepare a list of the parts in consultation with the various engineering departments, ready for the next race, and there I am

responsible for supplying them to the race team as they are needed.'

And during the races he is the support crew member for the refuelling operation, something he describes as, 'demanding but very exciting.'

When the race is over, Giovannini and his team immediately start to pack away the equipment, a job that is usually completed by 9 o'clock in the evening. At 6 o'clock the following morning it's time to start back to Maranello, where the trucks will arrive by the Tuesday evening.

It's a way of life that appeals only to a certain type of character, and much of the work is taken for granted and therefore goes unnoticed by most people. 'Of course you have to enjoy doing it,' Giovannini says. 'The hours and the distances are all part of the challenge of helping the team perform. I am used to it by now, but despite the years I have been doing it I have kept the same enthusiasm that I had on my first day. This is the kind of job that you can only do well if you have that enthusiasm – *la passione.*'

The professionalism of modern F1 is evident in this shot of the Ferrari pit. The corporate identity is just another thing that has to be taken to and from each race, and which has to be dismantled in moments once the race has finished – particularly at tracks such as San Marino, Hungaroring and Monza, where Ferrari victories frequently lead to an intrusive wave of delirious tifosi.

Sitting quietly in the background, Austrian engineer Gustav Brunner was tasked with interpreting Barnard's cars and honing them on the track.

Monza. It was a heartening index of the progress that the great Italian team had finally been making since the restructure.

The biggest step in 1993 had been the arrival of Jean Todt, who quickly began to reshape the structure of the race team, and to instil discipline, organisation and self-respect. As improvements in performance crept in for 1994, morale was boosted as the team tried desperately to believe again in its ability to win. Berger's Hockenheim victory that season paved the way for further improvement from the black horse which, if it wasn't exactly prancing yet, was at least back on its feet and trotting around. Although Benetton had made a lot of serious progress as Michael

Schumacher won a controversial fight for the World Championship, the Williams-Renault drivers Damon Hill and David Coulthard, and engineers Patrick Head and Adrian Newey, made no secret of their concern that Ferrari might soon be reaching fever pitch. It had, after all, the biggest budget of any F1 team, and if that budget was managed properly success surely had to follow. With di Montezemolo and Todt in charge, Head and Newey had few doubts that the money would be spent sensibly. They were right.

For a while it even seemed that Berger might have won the Brazilian GP, which opened the 1995 season, until Schumacher and Coulthard, first and second on the road, were reinstated after initially being thrown out for alleged fuel infringements. Berger was eventually classified third (to his relief, because he hadn't wanted to win in such a fashion), while Alesi was second in Argentina, fighting Hill and beating Schumacher. Shortly after the San Marino Grand Prix early in May, Berger expressed his optimism for the future. 'The Ferrari revival is no miracle,' he said, 'It is the fruit of two years of hard work. Reliability is good, and all we need is a little bit more power.' He was confident that by the Canadian Grand Prix in June Ferrari would be wholly capable of fighting for race wins with Benetton-Renault and Williams-Renault.

Alesi, who had shown so well in Argentina, Imola and Spain, echoed his feelings. 'Our new engine needs new features,' he counselled, having spent much of Imola trying vainly to pass David Coulthard's Williams and Barcelona chasing Schumacher's Benetton. 'Especially better acceleration. But it is just a question of hard work and getting things moving quickly at Maranello …'

Todt, an acute man who rarely misses a trick but is not given to flights of fancy, sensed the rising feeling in Italy, and also scented the imminence of success. More than anything, he appreciated the excitement it was creating among Ferrari fans the world over. 'Like everyone else, we can feel it,' he said. 'We have seen the results in the lap times and the progress of the team, which is much less different than it was before. I think Gerhard is completely right on this subject. He has his feet on the ground and he knows where we are.'

Within the sport there was a genuine well of good feeling that the red cars were running back at the front after the years in the wilderness, and few seemed to doubt that a Ferrari revival was good for motor racing. You just had to watch the way the tifosi behaved in Imola or Monza, and you began to understand that this was not just fashionable xenophobia as it so often is in other countries, but that support of the great team really is literally an article of faith to thousands of Italians who truly love their motorsport.

In June, on his 31st birthday, Jean

Berger took Ferrari back to the winner's circle for the first time since Spain 1990 when he won the 1994 German GP at Hockenheim. The wooded track's long straights proved particularly favourable to the 412's 800bhp V12 engine.

Back in 1992 Lauda had suggested that it would take at least three seasons for Ferrari to get up to speed, but the aftermath of Ayrton Senna's fatal accident imposed a revised set of regulations for 1995, which included a downsizing to three-litre engines.

Alesi finally made the breakthrough and won the only Grand Prix so far in his career, when Schumacher pitted with an electronic problem and the Ferrari swept its driver home to an emotional success.

'Honestly, there were times in my career when I said to myself: "I don't know what I did to God,"' he said as his eyes glistened, 'because I have had so many opportunities to win but didn't make it. But it was not possible to win before. I never got a car like this. It is unbelievable for me and for Ferrari. Finally, I won, so maybe now my life will be easier.'

He was entitled to feel a little lachrymose as finally he seduced a fickle mistress, for his maiden Grand Prix win had finally come at the 91st try, the longest any driver had gone at that time before being first past the chequered flag. That triumph was a profound experience for a mercurial man who had nearly been sacked the previous winter as Todt began to despair of his penchant for speaking his

Barnard's 412T2 was another beautifully proportioned car, and probably handled better than any other in extremes, but lacked the sheer downforce of its Williams, Benetton and McLaren rivals.

Though Berger and Alesi remained as Ferrari's pilots, one other star had a brief outing. Former Ferrari racer Carlos Reutemann (centre, with Bernie Ecclestone and di Montezemolo), drove a 412T in a demonstration at the 1995 Argentine GP meeting. He had been retired for 13 years, had never driven a semi-automatic gearshift before, and it was wet, but he was as brilliant as ever.

mind too clearly and wearing his heart on his sleeve too often. But the irony was that it had come without the revised engines and aerodynamics which had been expected, following delays after the various accidents in Monaco. In the end, Alesi's win owed much to the misfortune which befell Schumacher's dominant Benetton and the vagaries of the refuelling strategy which played in his favour and against Berger. But until he had been advised to conserve fuel, it was telling that Alesi was holding the gap between their two cars constant.

Certainly, the Williams-Renault team – and Damon Hill in particular – watched Ferrari's performance with growing unease. After Williams had dominated the first three races, Benetton had bounced back in Spain in May. Now, the indications in Canada suggested that Ferrari had pulled alongside too.

Crucially, both Benetton and Ferrari had something Williams did not: reliability. Suspension failure cost Hill the Brazilian Grand Prix, and in both Spain and Canada an electronic problem cost him the damage-limitation points he needed to amass while he awaited a more competitive car. 'The party is over,' he had said in Spain as Schumacher sprang back with pole position, and an unchallenged victory. And now Ferrari, too, had gatecrashed another.

As Ferrari's challenge appeared to gather strength, di Montezemolo spoke cautiously of mounting a full championship challenge in 1996. Todt, even more cautiously, preferred to talk of 1997. Barnard smiled with unalloyed relish as he considered the performance of his 412T2 chassis. All three knew that they might just win in 1995, if fate dealt them a decent hand.

'Many of the programmes I've done end up in three-year cycles,' Barnard said. 'The payback doesn't start until the third year. At Ferrari, I think we are beginning to see that payback.' His smile broadened as he added: 'And it is fantastic that this early in the season I am able to start looking seriously at our 1996 car ...'

Alesi's win put Ferrari back ahead of McLaren in the all-time winners' stakes, with 105 victories. And even Benetton and Williams weren't betting against more triumphs for the Prancing Horse as 1995 unfolded. Yet somehow it never quite came together again. At Monza, Alesi and Berger seemed to be heading for a 1–2 result, but then the camera from Alesi's car fell off and incapacitated Berger's. Then Alesi's car began to smoke, and Johnny Herbert swept through for victory. Later still, Alesi came within an ace of winning the GP of Europe at the Nürburgring, before having to concede victory to Schumacher.

The previous year at Monza Jean had stormed into the Ferrari pit after losing the race, thrown his crash helmet at

At the time of this book's publication it had only happened once, but Canada in 1995 finally gave Jean Alesi the reward he deserved when he won his first Grand Prix. It was an enormously popular triumph, and came on his 31st birthday. Here, having run out of fuel on his slowing down lap, Jean gets a lift back home from Schumacher, the man who would replace him at the end of the season.

the wall, then departed in great dudgeon with his brother Jose, apparently headed for the airport. Instead, he kept his foot buried to the floor and drove all the way back home to Avignon. It was an episode that illustrated the Latin side of his Franco-Sicilian nature, and another example of why Todt's patience was waning. He and Gerhard Berger had flown the Ferrari flag with great diligence, but for 1996 di Montezemolo and Todt were hatching exciting new plans that centred around Michael Schumacher.

The reigning World Champion needed no introduction. Since his stunning debut for Jordan at the Belgian GP in 1991, he had quickly established himself as the new star. With Senna's death in 1994, he had taken over the Brazilian's mantle as the greatest driver racing. Signing him was not just a major coup for Ferrari, but to its rivals a worrying indication of the underlying seriousness of its campaign.

To partner Schumacher, Todt chose Eddie Irvine, the maverick 30-year-old Ulsterman whose Grand Prix debut two years earlier had been punctuated by a punch from Ayrton Senna. As a small boy growing up in Northern Ireland, Irvine used to ride for miles on his bike just to look at a Ferrari parked by the side of the road. Now, the brash young driver had already been successful enough racing in F3 and F3000 to afford a Ferrari 288 GTO of his own. He had already brought himself to Ferrari's

Jean Alesi was born to drive for the Prancing Horse but for a number of reasons he never achieved the level of success that combination promised.

attention when, while racing for Jordan at the 1995 Argentine Grand Prix, he had approached Luca di Montezemolo and only semi-jokingly tackled him about a discount for spare parts for it.

Those who knew Irvine knew that

Ferrari hadn't picked him out of the F1 pack for his diplomatic skills. It liked him for his speed, his consistency and his courage – and the kind of abrasiveness that had earned him that left hook from Senna. Typically, Irvine did not hesitate after signing, to point out that he was still waiting for that discount.

He was there as number two to Schumacher, and he said, 'I accept that all the effort has to go into Michael at this stage. We are behind and we have

The future has indeed been brighter. Left, Jean Todt, Michael Schumacher and Luca di Montezemolo discuss strategy at Suzuka, 30 October 1998, while below, Schumacher, prepares to win pole.

to catch up. I'm here for two years, and Ferrari is going to give me everything they can to enable me to be right behind Michael. I won't be able to win if he is lying second, but I accept that.'

Other things were changing, too. Ferrari, for so long wedded to the concept of the V12 engine, had a new V10 on the stocks for 1996. Barnard had long favoured the concept and had

even once tried to persuade Maranello to look at British engineer Brian Hart's similar unit. Most observers regarded the V10 as the best compromise for the 3-litre formula which had come into being at the start of 1995, and some suggested that the Ferrari V12's inherent lack of torque at low revs, and its greater thirst, was too great a penalty to overcome.

'We are developing our engine,' Todt said. 'The V10 began bench testing in May but it has not yet been decided when it will race. That will, of course, depend on the results of these tests.'

There was more bad news for the opposition. 'We started designing the 412T2 before we had our feet firmly on the ground with our wind tunnel programme,' Barnard said. 'That's why it's fantastic that it has been going so well, and that it was so early in the season that I was able to start looking really seriously at the 1996 car. Assuming of course that nothing changes in the regulations before then, we can seriously arrive at a fairly well developed concept around the V10, and be sure that it is going to be fundamentally better.' Reiterating his three-year cycle theory he added, 'I am looking at 1996 as our 1990, a year in which we can have a serious crack at the World Championship.'

With Schumacher, a new engine and a dramatic new car, it was small wonder that Benetton, Williams and McLaren were beginning to take note of Ferrari once again.

Chapter 2

Politics
and passion

No team boss was ever more manipulative than Enzo Ferrari. From the mid-1960s onwards he refused to attend races, usually only appearing briefly and enigmatically during an early day at the Italian GP, his familiar dark glasses shielding the true thoughts in his eyes. Then he would fade away again, back to Maranello, where he would sit and think and plan, and await phone calls from his selection of lieutenants at the track. The 'Old Man's' wrath was best avoided, so these hapless trustees developed the self-preserving technique of telling Ferrari what they thought he would want to hear, and if necessary, disguising the truth to keep themselves off the hook as the scapegoat for his ire.

More often than not, this clandestine system worked against the drivers. John Surtees had his celebrated falling out with team manager Eugenio Dragoni in 1966 when the Italian consistently told Ferrari that his

protégé Lorenzo Bandini was being held back by the Englishman. In the doldrum periods in 1969 and 1973, when the cars were being annihilated by the opposition, the drivers were frequently blamed when the truth was that the engine and the chassis respectively were the true culprits. If men of the calibre of Chris Amon and Jacky Ickx could not make them go, it was crystal clear that the machinery was at fault, but that was not an easy fact to communicate to a man who prided himself on his company's engineering excellence.

Such practise persisted into the 1980. Gerhard Berger joined the team in 1987 to partner the Italian Michele Alboreto, who since 1984, had been Ferrari's blue-eyed boy. In 1985,

In the pre-Schumacher era, Ferrari's last serious chance of a World Championship had lain with Alain Prost, until the first corner of the 1990 Japanese GP at Suzuka ...

Alboreto had run Alain Prost close for the lead of the World Championship until Ferrari's development lagged behind McLaren's at mid-season. By the time Berger arrived, Alboreto's stock had diminished, and he was already on the receiving end of Ferrari's confidence-sapping polemics as Gerhard took his place in team affections. When his car rolled to a silent halt in Portugal in 1988, out of fuel, Alboreto watched third place disappear. He had driven the closing laps relying on the readout from his onboard instrumentation, and it had been wrong. 'Ferrari!', he barked. 'Even the computer is a liar!'

Even after Ferrari's, death Nigel Mansell felt that the internal polemics, upon Alain Prost's arrival as his team-mate for 1990, destroyed the superb relationship he had built up within the team during the previous season. 'As soon as Prost arrived,' he complained, 'he set about turning the team around to his own ends, soliciting the help of engineers and mechanics here and there. And the team was happy to let him get away with it.'

Within the sport it became accepted dogma that the polemics at Ferrari could never be stamped out, and that somewhere along the line they would always arise to stymie the team at the crucial moment. At first it had been because Enzo Ferrari operated his

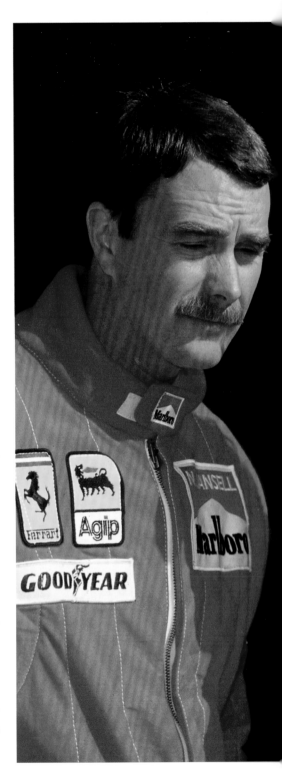

In the early 1990s Ferrari took no prisoners as the company adjusted to life without Enzo Ferrari. Nigel Mansell's relationship foundered upon Prost's arrival in 1990, while team manager Cesare Fiorio would be another who did not go the distance.

divide, diminish and rule style of management; latterly because, in his wake, subsequent managers feared for their positions and in turn did their best to muddy the waters in their own self-defence.

No-one suffered more from the clandestine atmosphere than Ivan Capelli who was recruited after Prost's dismissal at the end of 1991, to support Jean Alesi in 1992. Capelli was a splendid fellow, not at all Latin in his behaviour, yet fiery enough at the wheel to have given the dominant

Marco Piccininni, a former right-hand man of Enzo Ferrari, is still a familiar figure within the Ferrari organisation.

McLaren-Hondas a few scares in 1988, and to have pushed his Judd-powered Leyton House to the fore on subsequent occasions in 1989 and '90. The chance to drive for Ferrari seemed to be the break that would finally take him through to the big time. But Capelli was a fundamentally gentle character, the sort who had once tended birds hit deliberately by a rival team's van in Montreal. He was simply too nice a fellow for the harsh environment of the changing team, and for polemics that were as bad as ever they had been in Enzo Ferrari's internecine heyday.

'In 1992, I had very big pressure from the Italian media, because I was the first Italian after the Alboreto era,' he recalled. 'Everyone was extremely enthusiastic because Luca di Montezemolo arrived just after I signed the contract. The car was completely different, with its special double flat bottom, but unfortunately we saw technically from the first test that it had a very big problem ...'

Things began badly, and they didn't get any better. The team was in a state of change and it needed precisely what it hadn't got: a car that it understood. The F92A was too complicated.

'I realised immediately that the team was in a sort of reconstruction of all departments, because after Montezemolo, Harvey Postlethwaite rejoined. Everything was always in a new development. Every weekend we had new people, new strategy, new things, not the stability that you needed.'

Capelli made the mistake of trusting the wrong people. 'I was following too much the instructions from people inside who were telling me we had to work for the team. Later I realised that they were working just for themselves. I was thinking too much for Ferrari, and I should have worked just for myself to survive in a situation with such politics.'

By the fourth race, Barcelona, he realised that moves were already afoot to oust him even before the season had ended. Like many sensitive racers, he needed support not censure, and his confidence was shattered. 'There were some clear messages in the Italian newspapers, or things that happened to me concerning my private life. When I was talking to Postlethwaite or aerody-namicist Jean-Claude Migeot or to engine man Claudio Lombardi or even to Montezemolo himself, everybody was saying to me "yes, yes, yes", and in the end at the circuit the situation was always the same. Maybe the engineers would be working in a different way, or people would be managing the team in completely the wrong direction. They never changed, even if in private meet-

Two key figures brought back to prominent roles within Ferrari in the early Nineties were the men who had been the architects of its World Championship successes in the Seventies: Luca di Montezemolo and Niki Lauda.

ings they had said yes to this or yes to that.'

Going to Ferrari effectively destroyed Capelli's career.

Nicola Larini had a happier time, but admits that his role was subtly different as he began as Ferrari's test driver. 'It was no big problem to be a test driver for Ferrari. And even when I raced for the team, as a stand-in for Alesi in two races in 1994, I was still a test driver but now with a car to drive in a race. In my head there was no pressure.'

Larini was too politically astute to bite the hand that fed him his Sauber drive for 1997 by disclosing the extent of his anger with Ferrari when it chose Eddie Irvine instead of him to partner

Michael Schumacher at the end of 1995.

There is little doubt that the Italian media plays a crucial role in Ferrari's everyday life, whether people there care to admit it or not. Everything the team does is placed beneath a tabloid microscope, the way that the major football teams in England are kept within the glare of publicity. The situation is not helped by the presence of several daily sports newspapers in Italy which have regular space that needs to be filled. The Italian media can exert almost as much influence on a driver's career as the Ferrari team's management itself, and while dealing with that is part and parcel of a Ferrari driver's job, being Italian can make it

Jean Alesi always said that he liked Ferrari's controversial F92A with its twin-floor chassis, but it never realised what potential it might have had on the race track.

Like John Barnard, fellow Englishman Harvey Postlethwaite enjoyed two spells with Ferrari. In conjunction with aerodynamicist Jean-Claude Migeot, he was the father of the F92A.

all the harder, as Capelli discovered: 'The Italian newspapers unfortunately had a clear connection to Ferrari. They must have it, or they cannot get the scoop. And obviously if you don't have the scoops about Ferrari, you're not selling any newspapers.

'The thing that lets these people survive is when Ferrari is not getting any results. The day that Ferrari will win a championship, all these people will start to shake a little bit because having Ferrari in a non-winning situation, and performing inconsistently, lets these journalists follow Ferrari in a little mafia. Some are writing quite soft about Ferrari, while others are going direct to the point and maybe are attacking even the president, Montezemolo.'

Pino Allievi, doyen writer for the well respected *Gazetta dello Sport*, has frequently clashed swords with Ferrari management, and di Montezemolo in particular, by standing by his beliefs and always writing what he believes to be the truth. Not all of his fellow scribes share his courage or his scruples, however, and an incorrect story can soon be distorted further as others seek to embellish it in a vicious circle designed to disguise their maladroitness in missing it in the first place.

Alesi tried his hardest, but 1992 team-mate Ivan Capelli became just another victim of the polemics that seemed an inseparable part of life at Ferrari.

The Luca and Jean show

Marquese Luca Cordero di Montezemolo was born in Bologna on 31 August 1947, and left Rome University in 1971 with a degree in law. In 1973, he was taken on as Enzo Ferrari's lieutenant, overseeing the day-to-day running of Ferrari's racing efforts. At the time, its sports car programme was reasonably successful, but F1 was a disaster. The job was hardly a sinecure. Di Montezemolo signed up Niki Lauda and brought the hardy Clay Regazzoni back into the fold, and after a strong showing in 1974, he saw Lauda and Ferrari crowned as World Champions a season later. The red cars remained competitive until the end of the decade, and he moved on to become head of external relations of the Fiat Group. In 1981, he was appointed managing director of Itedi SpA, the holding company which supervises Fiat group's editorial activities, which embrace the daily newspaper *La Stampa*. Later, as managing director of Cinzani (another satellite of the Fiat group), he would organise the Azzurra challenge, Italy's first entry into the America's Cup.

From 1985 to 1990 he was general manager of the organising committee of Italia 90, as Italy staged the World Cup. And his career also embraced a spell as managing director of RCS Video, vice chairmanship of Bologna Calcio, and chairmanship of the Industrial Association of Modena. But late in 1991, mindful of the success of the 1970s, Fiat boss Gianni Agnelli saw him as the only logical saviour of Ferrari, a man with an intimate understanding of the company and its heritage. He brought him back as president.

Shrewd, urbane and possessed of an unruffled flair, di Montezemolo knew that bringing Ferrari back from the dead a second time would be no easy task, and that the prime requisite would be patience. He had arrived just too late to prevent the ludicrous waste of Prost's ability. Had he saved that situation, Ferrari might well have reached peak form sooner. As it was, his first goal was to lure Jean Todt away from Peugeot to spearhead the racing side of the operation.

Todt's credentials were impeccable. Born in Pierrefont on 25 February 1946, the little Frenchman gained recognition as a rally co-driver before masterminding Citroën's successes on the gruelling Paris–Dakar desert raid. He then switched in the early 1990s to run Peugeot's efforts in the World Sportscar Championship, culminating in victory at Le Mans in 1993. Only days later, on 1 July, he officially started as sporting director at Ferrari.

Todt brings uncanny calmness and searing intelligence to his role, allied to cunning and a capacity for detailed planning that is the envy of every other team. He plays a strong role in planning race strategy, but as ever, listens to inputs from all his lieutenants and is a notable exception to the old way of life at Ferrari: he takes a paternal role with his drivers. Of Todt, di Montezemolo says: 'I think he has done fantastic work. I like him because he has a very loyal approach, he is very straight, hard-working, and he looks at the interest of the team and of the name of Ferrari.'

Capelli does not hold the view one might expect, that the problem is that all of Italy wants to see an Italian winning for Ferrari. 'In Italy, if Ferrari wins a Grand Prix, Ferrari is winning. If Villeneuve wins a Grand Prix, it is Villeneuve winning, with a Williams. This is the little yet big difference, and you have to see this as a microscopic difference in interpretation. People are putting Ferrari in front of everything else, even the driver.'

So why is it that Italian drivers seem to get such a hard time at Ferrari? Capelli smiles in pained recollection of his time with a national institution. 'First of all because we are talking the same language of the journalists, and this is the big help of Schumacher and Irvine because they cannot have a direct connection with Italian journal-ists. So even if they are saying things in English or German, they cannot be misinterpreted so much by some Italian journalists the way that an Italian driver can be. In 1992, for instance, people were deliberately turning upside down my statements or my sentences.'

The situation was scarcely any more comfortable at times for the Englishman John Barnard, who had two periods as technical director at Ferrari. In his first, penning the inno-vative 639 for the 1989 season, Ferrari had yet to grasp the crucial importance of continuous development. Barnard could see that this was the way in which F1 would increasingly swing as the stakes increased annually, but had the devil's own job trying to persuade the company management. As the year

In his previous spell with Ferrari, Barnard had worked out of the appositely-named GTO organisation in Guildford, Ferrari's UK design satellite.

progressed his position seemed more and more tenuous. The crux of the problem was that Barnard's original deal called for him to be based in England, and indeed an offshoot was established in his adopted home town of Guildford. Appositely enough, it was called GTO, the type designation for some of Ferrari's greatest roadgoing sportscars.

The Italian media plays a crucial role in Ferrari's everyday life

'England is where I live,' Barnard said, 'and it is where my family is based.'

The situation worked well initially, until it became raddled with the inevitable politics. There were factions within Ferrari that harboured an intense dislike of any foreigner having an active involvement in the design of the cars. Sometimes Barnard felt that plans had been misinterpreted incorrectly; whether this was done deliberately or through genuine lack of understanding of the situation could not be pinpointed definitely. It all made for an uneasy situation, not helped by the Englishman's weak relationship with team manager Cesare Fiorio, who did not share his enthusiasm for an English-based design satellite no matter what it was called.

There is no question that Barnard not only dragged Ferrari kicking and screaming into the latest era of technology, but also that he had a direct influence on its development into a thoroughly competitive race team at this stage. The prospect of Alain Prost joining Nigel Mansell for the 1990 season created vast expectations, especially if Barnard was designing the car. This he did, but the internal pressures, and Ferrari's increasing insistence that its technical director should, after all, be based in Maranello, led him to split off to Benetton and Ford. In his place came Enrique Scalabroni, an Argentinian engineer who effectively inherited much of the work Barnard had set in train before leaving, and was then tasked with getting the best from it. It would become a familiar story.

Fiorio had risen to prominence in 1989 after a concerted attack by the Italian media had led to Pier-Giorgio Cappelli (no relation) being ousted. Once Gerhard Berger had announced midway through the season that he was off to take Prost's place at McLaren, he too became isolated.

Barnard's legacy first time around was to focus Ferrari's attention more and more on looking ahead. Its own 1.8-mile (2.9km) test track, Fiorano, within site of the main factory and right next door to the sporting operation, had been operational since 1972. Over the years it has steadily been updated, and although drivers often complain that it lacks really high-speed curves, it nevertheless provides valuable oppor-

The driver market was on the wane by September 1992, but by then the irrepressible Gerhard Berger had become the last driver for a while to pull off a multi-million dollar deal when he signed to return to Ferrari after three years with McLaren.

This time around, Ferrari assisted Barnard to set up Ferrari Design and Development, again in Guildford. (Sutton Motorsport Images)

tunities for private testing. Test drivers such as sometime F1 racers Roberto Moreno, Nicola Larini, Luca Badoer and Gianni Morbidelli have flogged round and round and round, clocking up literally thousands of miles of testing laps as Fiorano's closed circuit television and 44 photo-electric cell stations relay their car's performance via state-of-the-art telemetry.

Larini relates an amusing story which illustrates the lot of the Ferrari test driver. 'For me it was really important to drive a good car for a big company. I got so much experience! You can't imagine how many tests I did! Especially in 1993, when we were developing the suspension. I think I did nearly 9,000 miles!

'For me it was really more important to test a car like that, than to race from the back row. There was far more motivation to this solution, and also I could take part in touring car races, where I won my two championships. I was so happy to do that job, you can't imagine!

'I had no problems with the media, but after every test they tried to call me

Though FDD possessed all the ultra-modern CAD-CAM computer design facilities that any designer could ask for, Barnard also liked to create full-scale general arrangement diagrams on the drawing board.

Just how fast is an F1 car?

Have you ever tried to imagine just how truly fantastic the performance of a modern Formula One car is? Well, Michael Schumacher knows.

'It's difficult! With the F1 car you have more than 750bhp and a weight of 550 to 600kg depending on the driver. That's quite a relationship, and I don't know any road car which can give you this impression. So to answer the question, no, I don't think people can appreciate the performance at all!

'The Ferrari F550 works quite well in that direction and I just love it as a personal car, but still a Formula One car is a Formula One car.'

So that's the bad news for the Schumacher wannabes, but Ferrari and Marlboro wanted to find a way in which the massive gap in performance could be put into a meaningful perspective that everybody could appreciate. They took three cars to the Autodromo Enzo e Dino Ferrari at Imola, home of the San Marino Grand Prix in which Michael finished second for Ferrari in 1996.

First came Fiat's road-going hot hatch-back, the 20-valve Brava which is capable of around 130mph (210kph). Then the road-going Ferrari F550, a near-200mph (320kph) super tourer that is the spiritual successor to the legendary Daytona coupé of the 1970s. And, finally, the Ferrari F310 with which Schumacher won three races for the Prancing Horse in the 1996 F1 season. They also brought along three drivers capable of doing them justice: Ferrari test driver and touring car racer Nicola Larini; Schumacher's F1 team-mate Eddie Irvine; and Schumacher himself.

The plan was simple: match them all over one standing start lap of the 3.1-mile (5km) track, each starting at different times. It was the ultimate scratch race.

First, Larini donned his helmet and stepped into the Brava, the sort of car you can buy in any Fiat showroom. As Irvine began kitting up ready to drive the F550, Schumacher stood calmly catching up on the day's sporting news.

Off went Larini, pushing the Brava as hard as possible through every curve. After almost 30 seconds he had reached the Villeneuve Corner and off went Irvine from the startline. As his cloud of tyre smoke wreathed Schumacher, Larini was nearing

at home or in the car on the way home. And sometimes they tried to push me in some direction to arrive at the story that they wanted ...'

Not far away from Fiorano, near Florence, lies Mugello, which Ferrari purchased in 1988 and completely revamped to the highest standard. The 3.259-mile (5.24km) track remains active as a race venue, but it also doubles as an alternative test track for Ferrari.

Both tracks, incidentally, are used also by the roadcar side of the business, not just for prolonged testing but also for the Pilota Ferrari driving courses for owners seeking to maximise the potential of their cars, or to learn the art of controlling them at high speed.

Barnard's other legacy came after his

the Tosa Hairpin, a third of the way round the circuit. Dressed in his overalls but still bare-headed, Michael was calmly handing a mechanic back his copy of the day's newspaper. As he donned his helmet, Larini and Irvine were doing what they do best, throwing cars at corners, shifting gears at maximum revs, pushing as hard as they possibly could. Irvine had reached the Villeneuve Corner.

By the time the F550 was headed for Tosa, Schumacher had at last climbed aboard the F310, the tyre warming blankets had been removed and the engine fired up. Larini was by now half a lap ahead, having reached the Acque Minerale Corner. Irvine, catching him, was exiting Tosa. And this was when Schumacher scorched even more heat into his fat rear Goodyear tyres with a clutch-dropping racing start that etched twin black strips of rubber on to the tarmac. As Irvine reached Acque Minerale, Schumacher was already at Tosa, the Imola parkland echoing to the scream of his Ferrari's thoroughbred V10 power unit.

When Schumacher got to Acque Minerale, Irvine was further up the hill, at the Variante Alta chicane. Larini, meanwhile, was just going into the first of Rivazza's two left-hand turns. As the F550

clawed back the Brava's advantage, so it in turn was being reeled in by the F310.

As Larini exited Rivazza, Irvine was entering it and Schumacher was speeding through the Variante Alta. The battle had now distilled to a simple question. Could Schumacher get through the Rivazza in time to catch the two road cars as they sped towards the final corner and the finish line?

Through that final turn Larini clung tenaciously to his lead, but all the time Irvine was gobbling up the deficit, and, on the long run across the painted white boxes that mark out the grid positions, the F550's power and the laws of physics asserted themselves. But behind them Schumacher was coming like a red rocket that made both of them seem static. Irvine had only moments to savour taking the 'lead' before Schumacher went screaming by to take the chequered flag first, with fractions of a second to spare.

The Brava, a quick car by any standard, had started a minute ahead of him. The F550, one of the fastest road cars in the world, had been 30 seconds ahead. But the F1 car had caught and passed them both. The perspective could not have been drawn more convincingly.

second stint, when he rejoined together with Berger at the end of 1992. Once again an English-based satellite operation was set up, and again it was located in Guildford. By this time the Ferrari management had changed again, for Luca di Montezemolo had returned in 1992 as president.

He was smart enough to appreciate

that losing Barnard was one of the dumbest things Ferrari had done in a long time. He gave him permission to set up FDD – Ferrari Design and Development – and once again the plot began to move forward, although the potential gains were by now fewer as many of the lesser teams had begun to catch up with some of the front-runners. There were two potential

The clean-room facilities and the computer-aided manufacturing machines were the equal of the best English teams.

areas to exploit, however: active suspension, and aerodynamics. The two were inter-related. Barnard worked hard to build up the quality of engineers and engineering within the team, but was never totally satisfied with the wind tunnel testing that he was able to do. What he really wanted was Ferrari's own wind tunnel. His contract with the team expired in 1997 and, as once again the issue of the English technical base was raised, he decided to seek fresh challenges. Ferrari took the view that it had reorganised sufficiently to bring the technical department back in-house. Today, Barnard's second major legacy stands next to the main Ferrari factory, where 3,500 cars are produced annu-ally in the F355, 355 F1 Berlinetta, F355 and 355F1 GTS, F355 and 355F1 Spyder, 456M GT, 456M GTA and 550 Maranello ranges. This is the all-new wind tunnel which came on stream in 1997. It was designed by renowned architect Renzo Piano and can simulate precisely all the conditions the fullsize cars may meet on track. It is equipped with state-of-the-art data acquisition systems, both digital and analog, and the most advanced force-measuring systems. A 5m (16.4ft) fan creates the wind and requires 2,000kW of power, and scale models as large as 65 per cent can be subjected to any pitch, yaw and roll angles, and to steering inputs and dynamic movements as 300 sensors

If the Ferrari F92A was a disaster, the F93A was even worse as the company struggled vainly to close the electronic technology gap to Williams and McLaren.

measure the effects. The tunnel can also accommodate full-scale cars.

Ferrari was once cagey about its staffing levels, but di Montezemolo says between 420 and 430 people work at Maranello. Today, there is much less evidence of the feudal management policy so beloved by Enzo Ferrari. Di Montezemolo is president or chairman, with overall control. Enzo Ferrari's illegitimate son, Piero Lardi-Ferrari, is vice chairman, and Paolo Marinsek is managing director.

Jean Todt is in charge of the race team, as sporting director. He is responsible for planning the strategy of the team at races, and reports directly to di Montezemolo. Ross Brawn is director of engineering, responsible for co-ordinating the design, construction and track running of the cars, which are designed by chief designer Rory Byrne. Stefano Domenicali is the team manager, responsible for the day-to-day running and general race management, and Paolo Martinelli is in charge of engine development. Englishman Nigel Stepney is the chief mechanic, while Ignazio Lunetta is Michael Schumacher's race engineer, and Luca

Today the Ferrari factory is an impressive facility, located close to the company's own test track, Fiorano.

Baldisserri is Rubens Barrichello's.

In the past, Ferrari has often displayed an inherent inflexibility to change. Enzo Ferrari was one of the last manufacturers to join the rear-engined revolution of the late 1950s, steadfastly believing that the engine belonged in front of the driver. In later years, even into the 1980s, his cars were well behind others in chassis development until Dr Harvey Postlethwaite, the English designer responsible for James Hunt's Heskeths in the 1970s and latterly the managing director of Tyrrell, stepped in to bring its chassis design up to date.

Today, di Montezemolo and Todt have succeeded in removing such inflexibility and innate resistance to change, first with Barnard and latterly with Ross Brawn and Rory Byrne. The frustrations on the technical side with component supplies and working practises are a thing of the past, and Ferrari now habitually embraces new techniques without demur. Besides the dramatic new wind tunnel, Ferrari has every technical facility an F1 team could wish, including five-axis cutting machinery, autoclaves and four-poster test rigs. To some rivals, however, the cost has been a loss of its mystique.

Enzo Ferrari's house remains a lasting monument to the man who created a legend.

Many believe that, particularly since the transplantation of the 'Benetton Three' – Schumacher, Brawn and Byrne – Ferrari has simply become just another racing team, operating along the accepted lines of any other top team such as Williams, McLaren or Benetton. Some of the magic, they believe, has been a casualty of the winds of change. In that respect, perhaps such rivals betray themselves as traditionalists, as Ferrari continues to develop its new image.

'When you win you're a hero, when you lose they want your head'

Todt has no doubts that the technical situation is now at its best with everything back in-house. 'We have a real, proper organisation,' he says. 'I mean, when you have that it is better to achieve what you want. People are working together, talking together; there is dialogue between the engine and chassis people, so it makes possible a more comfortable situation.'

It also means that any problems can be solved much faster when people talk face-to-face. 'You know, it helps, but I would not like to do a comparison with the old situation. When that was done we had no alternative but to do that, but when it became more easy to achieve the whole organisation in Maranello, I did it. At the time we had the development department with John Barnard in England with FDD, it

was the right solution to have at that moment. But it was not the definitive solution. It was always a temporary situation.'

In 1998, he suggested that Ferrari was much closer to that definitive solution with its current set-up. It seemed to be working very well, with Ross Brawn and Rory Byrne fully settled in by the start of the season when their first car came on stream.

'Everybody is very settled,' Todt affirmed. 'Everybody knows what they have to do, so we now have a good organisation platform.'

He, like everyone else in the firing line at Maranello, has had to bear the repeated criticism of the media, and though Ferrari has had two very good seasons recently, there were moments in 1996 when the Italian media was demanding Todt's head on a platter with a fervour more usually associated with hate campaigns against British football club managers. At times the pressure on him must have been unbearable. 'When you win you are a hero, when you lose they want your head,' he shrugs with resignation and a short laugh. 'I try to ignore it as much as possible. And yes, I can actually do that. I sit in my office, within the company, and think of better things. My most difficult moments are during the race!'

The politics that once ate at Ferrari like a cancer now seem to be in remis-

A further inspired move was the recruitment of Jean Todt as sporting director of the Scuderia. He had arrived by the French GP in 1993, and would prove to be a key element in the complex jigsaw of Ferrari's revival.

Throughout the difficult years Lauda remained a source of down-to-earth advice. The lesson he preached most often was the need for patience, but it wasn't hard to see why Jean Alesi found that commodity hard to come by.

sion, the media apart. Todt is particularly pleased about this, you suspect, although he does not actually say so. There is no question that he has turned the team around, and its strongest rivals know this is one of the key elements which makes the team so dangerous these days. It can no longer be relied upon to beat itself. If, and it is a big if, the price of progress has been a slight loss of Ferrari's identity, then the cost has been worth-while, especially if part of that identity was based upon disorganisation and inbred means of self-defeat. Todt says that he has a good way of dealing with politics, and minimising them at all times.

'You need people to make politics, and I try to make other things than them. I keep everyone busy, and when people are busy we have less time to make politics.'

What nobody could have known in that season which brought yet another near miss, was that Ferrari still had a massive amount of work left before it could truly begin to reap the benefits of the changes di Montezemolo and Todt had brought about.

Chapter 3

Great expectations

It was inevitable that 1996 would begin with massive expectations both within Ferrari itself, and from the faithful tifosi. There had not been such an air of optimism since Alain Prost, also a reigning World Champion, went there for the 1990 season. In Michael Schumacher Ferrari had a man, like Prost, who had a proven ability to win races. And if the tifosi had been a little lukewarm when it was first announced that he would be leading the team, by the time the press launches had been held and the new car, the distinctive-looking F310, had been put through its initial paces at Fiorano, Berger and Alesi were forgotten men. All that mattered now was the 27-year-old lantern-jawed German in the red car which bore the apposite number one. Italy expected the World Championship at a stroke, and the now-retired Gianni Agnelli added fuel to the fire when he got carried away by the occasion at the car's launch and declared publicly: 'If Ferrari does not

win with Schumacher, it will be Ferrari's fault.' In the background, Jean Todt cringed.

By any standard the F310's debut in the Australian Grand Prix, which had switched to Melbourne and now opened the World Championship, was highly impressive. More impressive still was that Eddie Irvine outqualified the World Champion on their first run together as they lined up third and fourth behind the swift Williams-Renaults of pole-sitting newcomer Jacques Villeneuve and Schumacher's old adversary, Damon Hill. In the early stages, Schumacher gave notice of just what a pain he would be when he challenged the blue and white cars initially before retiring with a rear brake problem. Irvine soldiered on and brought his car home in third place. For a team that had doubted whether either of its machines would be strong enough to go the distance, this was indeed a respectable result that provided Ferrari fans with great encouragement.

Yet behind the scenes all was not well. The F310 broke new ground with its radical carbon fibre transmission, which needed more development, and Schumacher reported that the new car had far, far less forgiving handling than the interim V10-engined version of the old 412T2. Why then, the question was swiftly posed, had Barnard opted for an all-new car rather than developing what was clearly a pretty good concept with the old one?

On the face of it, it was not a bad question. Certainly, it was one for which the tifosi and the media demanded an answer, but they had varying ability to grasp the niceties of the situation. When Barnard tried to explain that the engine installation in any car has a critical effect on its performance, and that F1 was in the age of the completely integrated machine – and therefore an all-new car was precisely what was required not just for the here and now but for the long-term future – his explanations were instead treated as excuses. Already there was speculation that Ferrari would have to rush through another new car, but Todt poured scorn on that. 'We speak so much about Ferrari, and immediately it is magnified a hundredfold by the media. We have started developing the car, and the main structure of it and the engine, and we are doing all we can in the wind tunnel. But we have no intention of building another new car for 1996. We will try to optimise the project we have. But we are too far behind. Our goal is to be level with Williams.'

Schumacher went on to take a brilliant third place in Brazil, but that was all he had to look back on as Hill won the three opening events. The reality was that the F310 was not as good as the Williams. Nor, it was whispered, was it ever going to be.

For a start, it had been late arriving, partly because Barnard had deliberately chosen to optimise the design as much as possible within a very tight time schedule, prior to its construction, and partly because of technical

And here is the news. A delighted di Montezemolo announces Ferrari's plans for 1996 at the launch of the F310 in Maranello.

teething problems with the all-new V10 engine and its innovative transmission. 'If a new car is halfway right then you don't need a whole bunch of testing before the first race,' Barnard said. 'I'm quite encouraged by how the car went, though we certainly lacked something in terms of straightline speed.'

By any standard the F310's debut in Australia was impressive

Schumacher was clearly enjoying exploiting the depth of Ferrari's technical resources, which were fabulous in comparison with what he had previously experienced at Benetton, and he continued deliberately to play down expectations. 'I want to keep a realistic perspective on the team's position,' he said, repeating it so often that it became his mantra. 'The situation is that we had no testing in terms of development before the season began. We were able to do a little bit of work to sort out the worst problems, but there are still things which you have to change and adapt and make reliable. Whether we are going to find a lot more of those things, I don't know. We are pretty much on schedule, and I really want to take the first two or three races more as testing than to go for race results.

'Before Melbourne I didn't think we were in a position to think about good race results because we hadn't done a

proper race simulation with the new car. That's exactly the thing I expected when I came to Ferrari. But after the race I have to say that I was very encouraged, although I still think it is too ambitious to speak of challenging for the title this year. We still have a great deal of work to do.

'I am pleased about the principal situation at Ferrari. The base is all right; there are a lot of areas potentially that we can build on. I predicted that the gap between us and the front-running teams was going to be around a second in Melbourne, and that's what it proved to be. I have been surprised how well things went in the first month or so, because I didn't expect us to progress quite so quickly,' he admitted. 'That's good for my confidence, but of course we have to see how the first races go before I can truly draw any sort of conclusion.'

But he also had some other observations when pressed. 'Last year's car was very stable,' he said. 'But this year's is completely different. Basically we have a worse car, and we don't know why. Only Barnard can answer that question. I know he wouldn't have gone to all the trouble of building a new car if the data he gathered hadn't said it would be better, but maybe there is some problem in the car which we didn't find, or else whatever it was that he found in the wind tunnel hasn't translated on to the track.'

Irvine had greater cause for satisfaction with his Australian result, espe-

It took a while to get used to Michael Schumacher wearing the red colours of Ferrari and Marlboro.

cially after his heavy winter workload of test driving. The latter had come as something of a culture shock after the easygoing routine of life at Jordan. 'I'm enjoying being here,' he said, 'but I am surprised by the amount of work I have to do! For a little while there wasn't a lot because Michael was doing all the testing, but then they saw there was a need for me to do some. Even before my new car was ready I tested the old one with the new engine, and since then it's just been test, test, test.'

The reality was that the F310 was not as good as the Williams

---

Third in Melbourne really pleased him, after the lack of reliability he had experienced in all that testing. 'I was surprised that we were so quick there, to be honest. The engine was not performing as well in the car as it can do, we had a few bits and pieces we have to change there. And the chassis was nowhere near right. The balance was all wrong. It was very loose at the rear end going into a corner, very nervous; you had to be very careful with it. And there was a lot of understeer at the same time. It was a long way from being right. Yeah, I was pleasantly surprised!'

He liked the atmosphere within Ferrari, and already felt at home. And not surprisingly, given his podium finish, the team was quite pleased with its new number two. 'Everyone has

made me very comfortable,' he reported. 'All right, the attention is fully on Schumacher, but to be honest that's normal for me. The tension inside and outside the team is focused on Michael rather than on me, it's not affecting my performance at all because I get everything I need. The expectations are very high, but then so were Jordan's. Ferrari go into things in a lot more detail, because there are a lot more people here to do that. At Jordan there just weren't the number of people that Ferrari has. I didn't know what things to go into in great detail, to be honest with you. I've learned that here.'

He was getting on nicely with his illustrious team-mate, too, despite outqualifying him. As he described their nascent relationship, it was clear that he was choosing his words with greater care than he might have exercised the previous season with Jordan. He was, it seemed, maturing in his new job. 'I get on very well with Michael. I think we have a totally clear understanding between us. At the end of the day it's a lot easier to get on with someone. Being off the pace gets to you, you know. But you've just got to sit and work it out. Telemetry is a wonderful thing for doing that. It puts logic into motor racing. At the end of the day I'm not supposed to beat him. So there's no pressure, in effect. This is a very low pressure situation.

'I don't think there's much between us. He's definitely quicker than me at

Eddie Irvine, by contrast, had a history with Marlboro. The forthright Ulsterman soon fitted into his new environment.

Fighting colours

When knights went off to far-flung parts of the world in the old days, to fight for King and Country, they carried their fighting colours on their shields and their breastplates, or on pennants fluttering from their lances. It was the start of heraldry.

Today, a racing driver's crash helmet is his most instantly recognisable asset, an item of personal headwear that gives him an individual stamp that marks him out from his opposition even when he is flashing by a crowd at 200mph (320kph). It's a focal point around which his supporters rally.

For some drivers, the colours on their helmets simply evolved, with no particular rhyme nor reason. They were there simply to distinguish them from the competition. But for others there is a deeper significance.

Former Ferrari driver Jean Alesi wears his white, red and black colours as a silent tribute to the late Elio de Angelis, whose exploits with Lotus in the 1980s inspired him while he was starting his own career. The Brazilian, Pedro Diniz, patterned his helmet on the design of his fellow countryman, the late Carlos Pace.

Given the analytical approach that he brings to everything he does in a racing career that had by mid-1998 reaped him two World Championships and 31 Grand Prix victories, Scuderia Ferrari Marlboro team leader Michael Schumacher chose his distinctive red, black, blue, yellow and white helmet livery with great care.

'When I was starting out I had a plain white helmet,' he explained. 'But then a friend helped me to design something new. He had the idea to have the blue circle on top, and to decorate it with white stars. We chose the other colours together, and I've pretty much stayed with them ever since. I suppose they have become my identity, to an extent.'

That identity changed again in 2000, however. From Monaco onwards Michael sported a spiffy new paintjob in red, primarily to reflect the Ferrari/Marlboro heritage behind his driving, but also to distinguish him more for overhead onboard camera shots from team-mate Rubens Barrichello, whose helmet looked

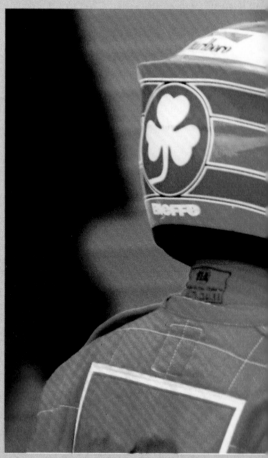

too similar with its blue skullcap.

Equally distinctive was the helmet of team-mate Eddie Irvine, who at that time, raced with orange, green and white colours. 'Like a lot of guys, I made do with an all-white helmet for a long time,' Irvine admits. 'But then I wanted something more spectacular. Back in 1989 I came up with that. I'm Irish, so the green stripes that I have are a reference to my home country. And, of course, I have to have a shamrock, don't I? It's another traditional national emblem, and that's at the back of the helmet.

'Then I had a kind of flame orange, which I used to joke meant that my helmet colours reflected both religious factions in Ireland and kept both happy. Now the orange colour is a bit redder because of Ferrari, and because I like the Prancing Horse of Ferrari so much, that's now on the top. Altogether, I think it's a pretty stylish design.' In 2000 he too changed, to a dark design reflecting his new role at Jaguar.

In days gone by knights bore colours on their shields. Today the drivers' helmets bear their own distinctive stamps.

the minute; in Australia our cars were a reasonable amount different, but I don't really know yet whether we like the same set-up. I drove his car at Estoril and I had no problem with it, but we just went down different roads because it was a test session. Melbourne was the first real testing I'd done, to be honest. I was surprised we

Schumacher's manager, Willy Weber, was a face that would soon become familiar to the Italians.

were so quick there when we were so relatively unprepared in comparison with Williams.

'I would say that Michael has an edge to consistency. I've always felt I can get a corner as good, if not quicker, than he can, but stringing them together has always been my problem. I think it's purely down to the lack of running in the car, but then I popped ahead. Hopefully I will keep that way!'

He wouldn't, but their relationship has gelled into something quite remarkable by recent F1 standards.

The workload in any major race team is enormous, and that was the biggest problem as Irvine tried to adjust to the sheer professionalism of running with a top-four contender. 'It just hasn't let up since January,' he reported. 'I've probably had four days off since then. I just haven't worked so hard in my whole damn life, you know? It hasn't just been hectic; it's been no real fun at all. The biggest thing is that I just haven't had any time to relax. I'd like to get a little bit of a break. But we're so far behind that we are playing catch-up at the moment.

'Don't get me wrong, I love being here at Ferrari, but right now I need to see where everything fits together here, so that I can sort out my life, make room for my life, so I can give myself a bit of space and relieve some of the workload. I'm hoping now that Melbourne is out of the way, and now that I have a third place under my belt, I can relax just a little. Right now, that's what I need.'

The massive expectations brought a pressure of their own kind, over and above those any racing driver experiences, but Schumacher had anticipated all of that because he could appreciate the tifosi's desperate desire to see Ferrari get back on top as soon as possible. He was shrewd enough to realise that Melbourne and Brazil would only add fuel to the bonfire of expectation. 'The tifosi are so vocal,' he would smile. 'Bringing the team back is a very big job, but that's precisely what attracted me in the first place. The challenge of it. When I came here it was a very emotional day, one that made me realise just what Ferrari means to the Italians, and to motor racing. You can feel the emotion behind the cars. It is there whenever you walk through the factory.'

Coming from the man that Ayrton Senna had described as an unfeeling, unsentimental automaton after he had watched him sit unmoving through a Tina Turner concert in Adelaide some years earlier, this was a remarkable revelation.

Schumacher believed even at that early stage that Ferrari could win races in 1996, but he remained innately cautious, knowing that the time would come and that there was no point to keep fanning the passion of the tifosi and the media. Astute in and out of the cockpit, he knew only too well that failure to realise expectations that he himself or the team might have fanned deliberately, would be met by a backlash of written and spoken criticism that would hamper the real effort to catch Williams. 'For sure I would like to win some races!' he laughed. 'But at the same time I must be realistic. I cannot even begin to guess how many I might win. But I do think that we will

Another new face in Maranello was Corinna Schumacher, whose easygoing temperament was instrumental in her husband's integration within the Ferrari empire.

have to wait until 1997 before we can start to think realistically about the Championship. It will be very hard for us to think of that in 1996, because we simply have so much work to do.'

Ferrari did win races that year. In

Elsewhere, Ferrari continued to benefit from the experience of former Honda engine guru Osamu Goto, who is now working on Ferrari-based engines with the Red Bull Sauber Petronas team.

faux pas on the wet streets of Monaco a fortnight earlier. 'I made a mistake, and I am very sorry for the team and very angry with myself,' Michael had said as he trudged home in the Principality, but there was no need for apologies in Barcelona as he thrashed his opposition with one of the greatest wet weather performances in history.

Overjoyed, Schumacher quickly took up a reporter's joke about driving King Juan Carlos of Spain around the Circuit di Catalunya prior to the race. 'Yes,' he beamed, 'he told me a few secrets of the track! And I would love to have him by my side in the Canadian Grand Prix as I'm sure he would bring me luck!'

He said that he felt that the circumstances had played into his hands. 'Circuits seem either to suit us, or not to suit us at present. At Monaco in the dry the car was perfect, but in the wet it was not good. Here in the dry we struggled, but in the wet the car was perfect. It seems to depend how high the level of grip is.'

Ferrari had won from the front, and all of Italy went berserk with pride. The success, however, would exert a hefty toll in the races to come, for the high simply served to make the lows that lay ahead seem even deeper. The Italian media was not slow to make that point.

If Todt wanted a low profile, the world had other ideas. It now expected the Prancing Horse to gather momentum and gallop forward on to Williams's tail. Instead, it stumbled in the next race in Canada, and fell badly in France and Britain, where early retirements drove the euphoria of

Spain Schumacher simply grabbed a wet race by the scruff of its neck and wrung out a brilliantly audacious performance that more than made amends for a very embarrassing first lap

Spain firmly into history. Ferrari was ravaged by a series of embarrassing early retirements centred on the engine and the carbon fibre casing of the innovative transmission which displayed an apparently ongoing reluctance to contain its lubricant.

'The car was just slow in Canada and Michael had a problem with all the brake balance being at the rear, so only the rear brakes were really working,' Todt grimaced. 'There was also a clutch problem which affected him during his refuelling stop, and which caused a halfshaft to break as he accel-

erated away. And the car was not quick in the straight; we have yet to understand why. We have not yet found the total reason. Michael did not have the best set-up, either, during the race. There were lots of little points.'

The French Grand Prix at Magny-Cours in June marked Todt's third anniversary as sporting director. To celebrate Michael gave him pole position, but there was a row with Williams over the legality of the aerodynamic barge boards behind the front wheels of Irvine's car, which thus had to start at the back of the grid. At least it started;

Right from the start, Schumacher introduced new working practices, and a whole new brand of dedication to his art.

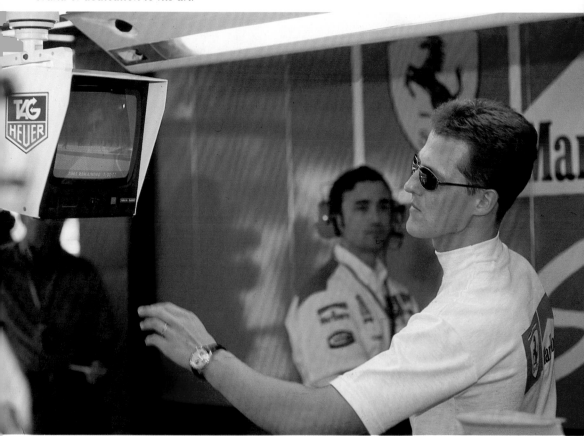

Schumacher's engine blew up on the grid formation lap. Worse was to come. Two weeks later at Silverstone, a hydraulic oil leak in the gearbox jammed Schuey's car in sixth gear and forced him to drive straight into his pit garage after three laps, while Irvine's car lasted little longer before it ran a differential bearing. The situation had reached crisis point.

Since Magny-Cours the Italian media had been screaming obsessively for somebody's head, and the witch-hunt was in full flow. Italian law demands that a culprit be identified in fatal accidents, and its media similarly demands a scapegoat when Ferrari underperforms. Todt was the man in the crosshairs.

There were myriad modifications in the pipeline for Schumacher to test, but where there had initially been talk that 1997 would mark Ferrari's true push towards another championship, sceptics already anticipated president Luca di Montezemolo's next round of promises that it would be yet another build-up year prior to an 'all-out assault' in 1998.

Spells in the doldrums are nothing new to a team that was in F1 even before the inauguration of the official World Championship in 1950. In 1954 and 1955 its cars were hopeless, and again in 1960 and 1962. In 1969 it

Barnard's F310 was an unusual-looking car that initially employed a droopy nose but would later wear the high nose that had become fashionable in Grand Prix circles. The biggest departure was the use of a V10 engine as F1 finally said ciao to the legendary V12. Left to right: Larini, Agnelli, Schuey, Luca, Irvine, Todt and a 355.

actually withdrew partway through the season to regroup, and that happened again in 1973, although each time it bounced back stronger and more competitive than ever. But the critics kept reminding everyone that it was a long time since Jody Scheckter won Ferrari's last World Championship for Drivers. Seventeen years, to be precise.

At Silverstone the mood within the team was one of complete astonishment. Technical staff voiced bewilderment, their stunned incredulity even embracing flights of fancy that outside agencies might have been at work. Schumacher, his long face set in a hard line, summarised it best. 'This is absurd,' he grated as he watched his World Championship prospects dying.

'We did a race distance testing at Imola recently, and again at Monza. We ran reliably here on Friday and on Saturday. And then we do three laps today. There is just no logic to it at all.'

The problem was that there seemed to be precious little logic to much of the Ferrari set-up.

'I try to ignore the pressure,' Todt said quietly. 'You know, in this game one day you are king, the day after you are nobody. We must stay with our feet on the ground, know exactly where we stand. We work, and ignore the external pressure.' And he made a telling point that showed just how far Ferrari had come as a cohesive team. No longer was there any suggestion of a driver growling protest at a lying

The tifosi didn't have to wait long for Michael Schumacher to weave his magic. Conditions during the 1996 Spanish GP were atrocious, but the reigning World Champion put Ferrari back on top with a stunning victory that set the church bells ringing in Marenello.

After the mid-season spate of engine failures, Ferrari hit back in Belgium when Schumacher raced to another great triumph, shrugging off worries about the steering.

computer. To his everlasting credit, Schumacher never at any stage, win, lose or draw, voiced even mild criticism of Ferrari. True, he was being paid a handsome stipend measured in millions of dollars, yet he never succumbed to the weakness of frustration and the temptation to let his true feelings slip out when things were going badly. 'Now if we win, we all win together,' Todt said. 'And if we lose, then we lose together. It is a team effort.'

And it had only taken half a season for that crucial relationship to gel.

But a team insider made the telling observation that in some respects Ferrari was suffering because it was not run along the same lines as British marques, such as Williams and McLaren. Both of them have cross-

pollination of ideas across all levels of the workforce. Despite the presence of di Montezemolo, and despite the commonsense Todt had tried to bring in his three years with the team, Maranello at that stage remained the hotbed of emotional polemics that it always was when Enzo Ferrari was alive. The Old Man's ghost still walked abroad in its corridors. The old hierarchical fiefdom remained and insiders insisted that only heads of departments were allowed to converse with the race engineers. Fraternisation was discouraged.

Tension had also been evident at times in the relationship between John Barnard's British-based design satellite, Ferrari Design and Development, and the engineering department at Maranello where Gustav Brunner and

Aldo Costa were employed to take what Barnard had created and run it at races. Both men had designed cars themselves, Brunner for ATS, Rial and Zakspeed, Costa for Minardi, and they had their own ideas and interpretations

'We test a lot, but we don't do it the right way,' another insider said. 'It's too disjointed and we don't have a baseline. There are many new parts to try, but we don't make enough of them. So those we have become unreliable. And now comes big shit.'

To his credit, Schumacher never voiced criticism of Ferrari

If a man of Todt's calibre couldn't make it work, Ferrari seemed to have little hope, for he was level-headed enough to harbour no illusion about the K2 the team still had to climb.

Fourth place for Schumacher on home ground at Hockenheim, behind not only the Williams duo but Jean Alesi in the Benetton, scarcely aided the situation. It was, indeed, a roller-coaster season, with patches of promise interspersed with dark moments. Todt maintained his customary even strain, refusing to be ruffled or to let the media attack deflect his concentration on what he had always known would be a formidable task. By contrast, the successes he had steered Citroën to on the Paris–Dakar, or Peugeot to at Le Mans, were mere children's games. The

season had both exceeded, and fallen short of, his expectations. 'I still feel that we are not yet where we need to be,' he said with masterful understatement.

'We are still facing too many problems. If you want to pretend that you can fight for the World Championship, then you must be in a position to score points with both your cars at every race, and this is not yet the case. Those are the negative points.

'But there are positive points too, if you think where we were a couple of years ago. Now we are protagonists. We are second in the Constructors' championship, and third in the Drivers', and we have the best driver with us. We have a new 10-cylinder engine, and things are going quite well. We have good potential. The car is quite competitive. But for me we are not yet where I want to be.'

He went on to quantify Ferrari's problems. 'First of all, we arrive quite late, so we have not done a lot of testing, and then we have had a few problems with an oil leak on the gearbox, as is well known. Things like that have not put us in the best situation. We were one month late, so we have to try to catch up the time. Nevertheless, Formula One is very demanding, and we are all working hard to have big potential. We are looking to close the gap, but you must not forget that we are the only team to build the engine, chassis and gearbox. We have no help from an engine supplier, who can just turn up with another engine and some mechanics. Everything we do is done in-house, though that perhaps gives us bigger motivation.

'That is one point. The other is that I don't want to use the excuse of being late, but we have had to rebuild our whole structure around a new engine, and that takes time. Some other teams struggle to reach and stay at the highest level. We need to be a strong team.'

Schumacher apart, the new V10 engine had proved to be one of the best assets, generally delivering good horsepower and more reliability than many had anticipated, notwithstanding the mid-season problem with the quality control of pistons. The latter was a deep irony for Todt, who had said in Canada during a conversation about the engine's impressive performance: 'I don't want to be superstitious. I don't want to say that I did not expect to be as competitive as we are on the engine side from the beginning, because I am always scared that we might blow up an

Jean Todt said that winning two Grands Prix in 1996 was a dream, but things were about to get even better for the Prancing Horse when Schumacher raced home the winner in the Italian Grand Prix at Monza. It was Ferrari's first win there since Berger's in 1988.

engine in ten laps. It is not yet fantastic! I want to wait until the end of the year before I make the point. But so far the situation is quite good.'

We are the only team to build the engine, chassis and gearbox

The German GP was a turning point, although it was not appreciated at the time. There had been a new aerodynamic package which was expected to improve the car on low downforce circuits such as Hockenheim, but although it disappointed there it proved extremely promising at the next race, at the Hungaroring, ironically one of the highest downforce tracks on the calendar. There, Schumacher chased Villeneuve until his throttle unit gave problems. Then came Spa and another great victory.

Schumacher's Belgian weekend began badly with a serious accident in practice on Friday morning, but he fought back. 'I had exactly the same thing last year,' he shrugged. 'So I thought maybe it was a good omen! But like I said in Spain, after the gap between us and Williams in qualifying I wouldn't have bet one penny on my chances of winning. What we managed was really fantastic!'

Indeed it was. The 21st Grand Prix victory of his career was not achieved without a measure of concern, however, because at one stage he was worried about a problem with the Ferrari's steering. 'At half distance I was scared I might have to stop because I was pushing very hard behind Hakkinen and the way to be quick was to go very hard over the kerbs. The steering took a knock which made the car very strange to drive – especially at Eau Rouge. The car felt a bit loose, but the team told me over the radio that if I stayed away from the kerbs there would be no danger and I wouldn't have any further problems. I regained confidence and everything went well.

'There was no way, I thought, to win. I was more thinking to finish and get some points. What we managed to do today was really fantastic. Even if we were not quicker than the Williamses, we were able to keep their pace and we won by doing everything right – the set-up, the strategy and the pit stops. I always intended to make my fuel stop on lap 14, and it was coincidental that this was when the safety car came out because of Jos Verstappen's accident. That was our strategy, and in any case, the fuel tank was telling us to do it, because there wasn't enough fuel left for another lap!

'The only similarity between this win and Spain was that they were both unexpected. In Spain I won with a big margin as a result of the weather conditions. Here, I won in the dry and had to fight all the way to the end. This is a really important win for me and the team after all the problems we have had. For me it is like something from Hollywood.'

For Todt, too. 'We need to win one more race,' he had said after Spain. 'That would make me happy, because it would be one more than we have won in each of the last two years. If I have a dream, it is that we win another one ...' Now Ferrari had. On the rostrum he celebrated with Schumacher and Olympic athlete Michael Johnson. Manager and driver embraced and kissed as the smaller man clutched the winning Constructors' trophy and slicked down hair soaked by the champagne shampoo the champion had administered. Todt tried unsuccessfully to wipe the stinging alcohol from eyes already wet with tears. Later, his admiration for the German knew no bounds. 'Michael is the World Champion, and a fantastic driver,' he said. 'He is very professional, very motivated, he has very good spirit. And he is a very hard worker. He is a point of reference for the team, through what he has given. He is not a technical director, like some people pretend he is, and he very much needs the support of the team. He gets all we can give. He is a driver, and he is all the things I have said, a great guy. He loves driving, and for us it is fantastic to have him. The other side is that he

Like Enzo Ferrari before him, Luca di Montezemolo was not a familiar figure at races. He made a rare appearance at Silverstone for the 1996 British GP, only to watch Schumacher retire early with a broken engine.

All work and no play … Schumacher, Irvine and test driver Luca Badoer enjoy their moments of relaxation when they come, be they …

deserves a good car and a good team; if he doesn't have that, he cannot work. He is very curious; he wants to know and understand, but he needs technical support, as much as we can give.'

At Monza that September Schumacher worked his way into the hearts of even the most resistant tifosi when he delivered Ferrari's first victory on its home ground since Gerhard Berger and Michele Alboreto had finished first and second there only days after Enzo Ferrari's death in 1988. While Hill spun after clipping one of the stacks of tyres mounted controversially in Monza's numerous chicanes, Schumacher stalked Alesi's leading Benetton, and benefited from two stunningly fast laps while the

Frenchman was refuelling, to grab a lead which he retained even after his own stop. It was textbook Schumacher stuff, the reason why he was worth every penny of the rumoured £16 million salary Ferrari and Marlboro had jointly stumped up for him.

There had been much speculation about Eddie Irvine's future for the majority of the year, despite Ferrari's indications that he would be staying with the team for 1997, partly because he had upset the Italian media even before he sat in a red car by telling them that he didn't really care what was written about him because he had never met a journalist who knew what

… snowboarding …

... skiing ...

he was talking about. At Monza, Todt finally laid all of this nonsense to rest when he reiterated his wish to retain the Ulsterman's services. Michael liked him, they got on well together, and after a string of retirements he had got his act together with a fifth place finish in Portugal. It all made sense not to upset the status quo.

'Eddie is in a very difficult situation, you know,' Todt explained, 'because he is the number two driver. He starts each race with exactly the same car as Michael. In between races, Michael has priority in testing. Eddie is facing the best driver at the moment doing all the testing, and has to fight against him for the team at weekends. It is very difficult, and he needs a very strong spirit. As a person Eddie has that strong spirit. He is a charming guy for the team at the moment.'

There were no further wins, but third in Estoril and second in Suzuka cemented a comfortable third place in the Drivers' Championship for Schumacher. It was a start, but it wasn't what he wanted to stay happy. The bare facts did not make impressive reading. Hill had scored 97 points, Villeneuve 78, Schumacher 59. Williams-Renault's 175 points was more than double Ferrari's 70. Between them, Hill and Villeneuve had won 12 races and taken 12 pole positions; Schumacher had won thrice and was quickest in practice on four occasions.

Where 11 times a Williams had set the fastest race lap, only twice was a Ferrari the best. Where Hill led for 1,356 miles (2,183km) or just over 47 per cent of the race laps, Schumacher's tally was only 370 miles (596km), or 11.4 per cent. And everybody knew he was the best driver in the world, even if ego prevented some from acknowledging the fact.

With its healthy contribution from Marlboro, not to mention Fiat's financial injections, Ferrari's annual budget was estimated to be the right side of £60 million, yet here were

... or snowmobiling.

Williams and Renault making a monkey of the Prancing Horse on probably just over half of that. But perhaps the greatest irony was that while internal factions at Ferrari, and the media, were all arguing over this shocking imbalance, Frank Williams himself was quite open about how apprehensive he felt every time he thought about the sheer scale of Ferrari's challenge. He probably believed more than many tifosi that it really would be only a matter of time before the Italian team wrested away his cars' position as pacesetters.

Jean Todt, meanwhile, understood that even with such an expert rider as Michael Schumacher the Prancing Horse had to be massaged into a canter before it could be spurred to gallop again, but others were less patient and had less realistic expectations. Agnelli's comment, 'If Ferrari does not win with Schumacher, it will be Ferrari's fault,' continued to haunt the team.

Todt tried to ignore all the silly talk and continued gearing up for 1997, and as the disappointed fans licked their wounds, he knew that it was unlikely to be Agnelli's silver-haired head which dropped into the executioner's tumbril if the old nag did not begin to exhibit very soon the long-term capability to metamorphose into a race-winning thoroughbred. One way or another, 1997 would be a crucial season.

Chapter 4

Getting
the mix right

As he planned Ferrari's 1997 World Championship assault, and addressed its shortcomings of the previous campaign, the upper-most consideration in Jean Todt's mind was not just to get the car right, but to get the right mix of people. Traces of the old polemic society within

Ferrari's new car for 1997 was unashamedly a copy of the successful high-nose Williams FW17 and FW18 models, for that is what di Montezemolo and Todt wanted Barnard to create.

Maranello had to be eradicated. If that meant surrendering what some saw as part of Ferrari's heritage and identity, that was just too bad. Winning meant moving with the times, and if that meant making Ferrari more like the other leading British teams – Williams, McLaren and Benetton – then it was a price worth paying.

Thus it was a very different-looking team which was unveiled to the media at the traditional launch of the new car at Fiorano in late February. Barnard's contract was about to expire, and Todt was adamant that he wanted the technical leadership based within Maranello. So he had approached both Ross Brawn and Rory Byrne, the king-pins of Benetton's technical infrastruc-

ture. He outlined the team's reasons for relocating its design department to Maranello as part of its revised strategy.

'The '97 car is not one man's car, it is a Ferrari car. Of course, John Barnard has helped in the design, with a lot of other people working on it. This decision was made very carefully, and before taking it we needed to have the structure, which is now a very strong one, in Italy. Of course, to give Ferrari the fruit of it, it takes time. If you put some seeds in the earth, before you get the flowers it takes a few months. For us it will take a certain time. We know that, and we are prepared, and already I think we are in the right direction.'

Ferrari was negotiating the sale of the FDD facility to Barnard, who by that

The F310B neatly packaged an improved version of the race-winning V10. Both Barnard and his successor Ross Brawn were adamant about the crucial importance of total integration of the car's components.

stage was no longer directly involved with development of the F310B.

The previous season, di Montezemolo had stressed the importance of Ferrari maintaining a presence in the UK, F1's 'Silicon Valley'. 'Yes, it is obvious, because most of the teams are British,' agreed Todt diplomatically. 'But I think we did quite a big work bringing very good people to Maranello. It has taken me three and a half years to be in a position to achieve that. So I think now that we have a very strong team there, though saying that we are working with suppliers in Japan, Germany, France and UK. There are very good suppliers in the UK. So what was true six months ago, is still true today, but completely we are in a position now to have very good people working in Maranello. For us this is very important.'

Brawn, at that time 38 years old, had started in F1 with Williams, but had also had spells with Beatrice Haas Lola, Arrows and TWR, before switching to Benetton. He was a typical product of the British racing car industry, a large bespectacled man with an owlish mien who specialised initially in aerodynamics but graduated to draw complete cars before taking on the role of technical overseer.

Byrne had risen with Toleman as it rose from F2 to F1, designing its cars and continuing to do so after the takeover by Benetton in 1986. Beyond a brief spell with Reynard's stillborn F1 project in 1991, he had an unbroken alliance with Benetton which was instrumental in the team's rise to prominence in 1994.

Unlike fellow countryman John

Into Barnard's place as technical director came Ross Brawn, the fortysomething engineer with whom Schumacher had worked so effectively at Benetton. With him came that team's chief designer, Rory Byrne.

Barnard, whose five-year contract with Ferrari was about to expire, he had no qualms about uprooting himself from rural life in England and transplanting to Italy.

Schumacher: 'fatherhood has changed me for the better'

Fatherhood seemed, if anything, to make Michael Schumacher even faster, to judge from his performance during the 1997 season.

The German's winning run round the rain-soaked streets of Monte Carlo may have elevated him temporarily to the lead of the Formula One World Championship, but as far as 28-year-old Schumacher and his young wife Corinna were concerned they had already won the biggest prize of all earlier in the season when their daughter, Gina-Marie, was born.

Michael admits that the birth of his first child changed his outlook on life.

'Becoming a father has had an effect on me. Before, Formula One was the whole focus of my attention, but now it is family first and then motor racing.

'I enjoy being a father. I was there at the birth, and it was an emotional and very special experience, as I am sure it is for any father. And it was tiring work sitting up at night nursing our daughter when I returned from the first race in Australia. Tiring – but wonderful!'

Parenthood can change some drivers, taking the edge off their performance. But Schumacher insists he has only changed for the better.

'Becoming a father did not suddenly make me more aware of the dangers of motor racing nor make me wonder how long I should continue. Two years ago, I said I would retire in five years but now I'm not so sure. It will depend when the day comes that I don't want to test and race any more. When you don't like to do

'I've obviously become a bit more of a European!' he chuckled. 'There's obviously a lot of travelling involved in Formula One, so that aspect's not too different, but I must say that Italians are very nice people. They've shown me a lot of hospitality, and I'm enjoying it very much. On the human side it's working very well.'

The decision to leave Benetton had been made the previous summer. 'There was a key time for me to decide whether I was going to stay or go to Ferrari. Nothing was tied up until later, but in my own mind that was when I had to decide. We were into the new car for 1997 by then, so there were

certain plans that had to be made for 1997/98 at Benetton. It was kind of reaching a crucial stage, where I felt I had to tell Flavio (Briatore) what I was going to do.

'It was time to move. I'd been at Benetton for five years, we'd been fortunate to win two World Championships, and I had to look at where my next challenge was. I'm sure there was a challenge winning again with Benetton, but there was an even bigger challenge winning another one with Ferrari. I guess also I was at the stage where I wanted a different culture, a different environment, just to try it. Because life isn't practice for something, that is the time to stop. You cannot predict when that might happen.'

Schumacher, the fitness fan who eats muesli for breakfast and watches his weight more closely than any oversized dieter, is one of the highest paid sportsmen in history. But while that means his family will never want for anything, he says that money is of secondary importance. To any successful athlete, it is usually only a measure of their value. 'It gives me satisfaction knowing I do not have to worry financially about the future,' he says. 'But to me, motor racing has always been more than just a financial thing. The racing is the most important part of it, not the money. People get the wrong impression. Sometimes the media build up people like myself as not human. But, of course, I am. When I am racing, I am focused on what I am doing. Maybe I am a bit more precise and professional than others. But that is my way. What I try to do is commit myself totally as a racing driver when I am working for Scuderia Ferrari Marlboro ... and then to switch off completely to devote myself to my wife and baby.' Early in 1999, Gina Maria was joined by brother Mike.

The Schumachers are also animal lovers. Corinna loves horse riding, and both were captivated by the stray dog that attached itself to them one year in Brazil. So much so that they went to the considerable trouble of adopting it and putting it through quarantine back home in Monte Carlo.

Brother Ralf, of course, is also in F1, and the two are regularly seen together. Michael helped him all he could in his first season, with Jordan in 1997, although some say the relationship has cooled a little as Ralf has got faster. Or, perhaps, since his Jordan landed on Michael's Ferrari on the first lap of the Luxembourg race in 1997, which in retrospect may have cost him the world title ...

the real thing. We're only here once, aren't we? I'm going to bust my balls trying to do it with Ferrari, but if it doesn't work out, it's an experience I wanted to have. And I'm sure it will work out.'

Schumacher obviously played a role in Brawn's decision, although he denies it was instrumental. 'He was willing to make the commitment to make it work in the long-term, which is what it needed,' Brawn related. 'It would have been very difficult for me if Michael was leaving at the end of the season. But he was willing to make a longer-term commitment, which is what I did as well. I'm here for three years.

'Michael was very fair. Naturally, he had an interest, and we had some discussions. But he knows me and we didn't have to discuss it a lot. With the right pieces in place he was willing to make a commitment ...

'He was very similar to me, in a way. He'd won two World Championships, and you keep going on winning them. He could have stayed at Benetton and maybe won some more, but how many do you need to win? Winning one with Ferrari is different to winning one with Benetton, and that's the same for me.'

Brawn took an apartment in Sassuolo, the town in which former F1 racer Andrea Montermini was born,

If Barnard looks a little wistful here it is understandable. Just as Ferrari seemed on the edge of launching what would prove to be a convincing challenge for the World Championship, for the first time in seven years, Todt decided that the design facility had to come back in-house at Maranello. Barnard did not want to work on that basis and left as his five-year contract expired. It was an amicable separation, however, and he purchased FDD from Ferrari, renaming it B3 Technologies.

and which is about ten minutes' drive from the Ferrari factory in Maranello. 'It's a very Italian small town, so you can go and have a walk on a Sunday morning, on the piazza, and everybody's there, milling around, having their coffee. It's very, very good. I enjoy it.' It's certainly quite a change from home in Henley-on-Thames, in England's middle-class Green Belt area.

For a family man, the new life has necessarily been something of a juggling act. 'My wife, Jean, stays in Italy in the week in between races and then goes back to England for the weekend of the race, so she's sort of half and half. My elder daughter, Helen, goes to university this year so she'll be off looking after herself shortly. And our younger daughter, Amy, is just doing her GCSE exams, so she'll be at an English school for another couple of years then probably come out and join us, or become a commuter, I'm not sure!'

A very keen fisherman, Brawn admits he didn't get much time for that sort of relaxation in his days at Benetton, nor since joining Ferrari. 'I fish on holiday, that's my release from the pressure of F1,' he says with ironic humour. 'We normally have a two or three-week break over the winter and I pick somewhere nice for the family, which also has some fishing! Holidays are okay for a little while, then I need to do something, so fishing fits in very well. Mauritius has been popular in the last year or two'.

Anxious to integrate as quickly as possible into the team, he immediately settled into two Italian lessons each

Brawn and Schumacher immediately picked up where they had left off, reforming their close bond.

week. 'It's a great language, and though I'm in the early stages I understand a little now.' He laughed and rattled off a string of phrases to underline his point.

Ross Brawn was extremely optimistic about Ferrari's prospects in the great team's 50th season. 'The thing that really pleased me,' he said, his enthusiasm evident in every gesture, 'was to discover on arrival that so many of the fundamental pieces of the technical jigsaw were already there. I think there is an image of Ferrari, from the outside, that is no longer valid. I don't know what it was like in the past, I couldn't judge. But I think that with Jean Todt as sporting director, and the arrival of Giorgio Ascanelli to head the racing side a couple of years ago, from McLaren, the thing is in much better

shape than people gave Ferrari credit for. What was lacking was a technical reference point at Maranello, and we've got that now that Rory Byrne has joined. That's great news, certainly a bonus. When I heard he was retiring, I thought we'd try pretty hard to twist his arm.'

Brawn reports directly to Todt, while Byrne has responsibility for the design of the cars. At the time Brunner was still in charge of development, although he would leave for Minardi at the end of the season. Byrne and Brawn, of course, had worked together with great success at Benetton, where their technical expertise had melded to perfection with Schumacher's fabulous skill to win two World Championships.

Barnard and Brawn did not overlap

By the start of 1997 it no longer seemed unfamiliar to see Schumacher kitting up for Ferrari.

during their Benetton periods, and this time any overlap was miniscule too. 'I think the fundamental principle of Ferrari and John's future had been agreed, so I came along after that,' Brawn explained. 'John didn't want to come to Italy; I guess he was asked and didn't want to, so people here decided what they wanted. I worked with him a little bit on the F310B because he came to some of the tests, and I must say I have had a very easy relationship with him, in slightly unusual circum-stances. If I wanted to know something I could ring him up and he would help me.'

Within Ferrari, the presence of a technical director and a chief designer at Maranello made things smoother. 'With Rory and I there people in the team could get their technical queries answered straight away. They could come to us with their problems, and get them solved. Often, it would be just a word of encouragement that they needed.'

Brawn's experience made him very strong on overall organisation of tech-nical departments, leaving Byrne free to concentrate on the pure design.

The former champion had been taken close to the hearts of the tifosi ...

'That's what I like to do,' Brawn explained. 'I'd love to design a car again, but I can't. If I get too heavily involved in that, something else would suffer so I have to try and keep a balance about the whole arena and devote my activities to whatever is the weakest area at the time.'

He felt like a kid in a candy store as he exploited the facilities at Maranello. Computational fluid dynamics, a key mathematical tool in the design process, requires a lot of number crunching and hence some serious computer power. When Brawn was at Benetton they came up with a novel solution to the problem of finding a sufficiently powerful computer. 'What we did was to run a lot of the stuff overnight and just link all the work stations, so we'd use all the processing power. So come eight o'clock at night when people were drifting home, as they turned their machines off we'd commandeer them and link them into the processing network. Of course we could have used a Cray, by buying time on it, but there were other ways, and all the Benetton equipment was effectively redundant overnight, so we used to organise ourselves that way.' But there was no need for that at Ferrari. Brawn grinned. 'We have some pretty powerful computers here!' It was another index to the armoury of a really top team.

The new technical director was also fascinated to see how the engine and

... and continued to bring an unrivalled intensity to his race preparations. Ferrari knew it was working with a real champion.

chassis departments integrated, and held the strong belief that you should really design the engine for the sort of car you wanted to build, rather than building a car around the engine you just happened to have. Integration was the key. At Ferrari, the engine people had historically tended to have their own problems, but now there was already a far greater understanding of the need not just for power but general usability, driveability and fuel economy, the integration of the whole package. An engine that uses more fuel is not going to be competitive. Even Ferrari, which by tradition was supposed to have the most powerful engines of any F1 era (even if that manifestly was not true in, say, the mid-1960s), had come to understand that having an engine which looks good on the dynamometer does not mean much these days. It's how the engine performs in the car and how it can be used by the driver that really counts.

There's a fair Italian element but it's always been open house

---

As the manufacturer of its own engine Ferrari had exclusivity of supply (the engines it supplies to Sauber are not to the same specification), but the downside is that it is more difficult for the team in terms of limited feedback. In 1997, for example, Renault could rely on the race-honed comments of

Jacques Villeneuve and Heinz-Harald Frentzen at Williams, but also Gerhard Berger and Jean Alesi at Benetton. Ferrari had only Schumacher and Irvine. Brawn made an interesting point. 'Renault really knows what's required because they talk to the teams. When I was at Benetton we spent a lot of time with Renault talking about what would happen if we did this or did that, moving away from just the power aspects. And of course they were getting the same from Williams. Now Paulo Martinelli and his people at Ferrari are doing the same with me. Engines are difficult, because they've got a longer lead time than the car. I mean, we'd be designing bits for the following year's engines as early as March the previous season. So it needs more time to steer an engine in a certain direction.'

Brawn also found interesting differences working in an Italian team compared with working in a typical British outfit. 'There is an element of working with a car company that also races, as opposed to working with a specialist team dedicated to only one end. But you just have to put that to one side. If it becomes a distraction then it's a negative element. I knew when I was going to Ferrari that these people have to respect the unions, so there's an occasional strike. People down their tools and off they go, because they're part of the union. You can't blame them for that, you just have to accept it. You can't challenge it or try to confront it, you have to roll with it. That's a typical side of Ferrari, but then being part of a car company you've got the huge resource within

Fiat, and I'm just starting to learn how we can use that. It's not something to get concerned about, because you're not going to change it.'

There was also the possibility that the Italians within the company, with their passionate belief in all things Ferrari, might take badly to technical direction from an Englishman and design inspiration from a South African. 'There's a fair Italian element,' Brawn concedes, 'but it's always been open house. If there's an Italian who can do the job, he'll get it.' There was not, he stressed, any pressure to hire Italians first, or to train up a whole new generation who would eventually succeed the interim foreigners. Ferrari, like most other teams, had gone far beyond such petty chauvinism and had fully embraced the cosmopolitan age.

'To be perfectly honest,' Brawn continued, 'Luca said to me, "If you can give an Italian a job then I'll be delighted. But if you can't find a good Italian to do the job then we'll have to find someone from outside to do it." So there's no pressure there. And if there is a good Italian to do it, why not? If the guy speaks English, knows the culture, it's much easier to do that. If it's a very specialist task, we may have to look farther afield. We've got stress engineers who are Italian, aerodynamicists. But equally, when I was at Benetton, we had people from all over the world, French, Germans, Italians. There was no barrier, and I don't think there should be in racing, or any big company.'

Schumacher's office, complete with map of Interlagos at the Brazilian GP.

Schumacher was delighted when his old colleagues stepped aboard, and believed that they brought immediate useful changes. Brawn was characteristically cautious. 'It's difficult for me to judge how Ferrari was last year. I can only judge on the basis of this year. We still have a lot of work to do, to improve some of the systems we have and one or two of the team's approaches. But it has helped a lot to have the technical direction located in Italy, I'm sure.'

Barnard's F310B was a sleek but conventional car reminiscent in appearance of Williams's successful FW18 model from previous seasons, and the evolutionary FW19. Inevitably stories emanated from its first tests in Fiorano that there were problems, for the Italian media needed to fan up the story. But although the car was much better than the F310, there were still things that needed sorting out. For a start it had too much understeer, which hurt the tyres as a race progressed.

'Cars are funny things,' Brawn ruminated in 1997. 'We're not going to change this one overnight. When you're competitive there's nothing wrong with them. And they can be the same car but somebody's going faster, and suddenly there's a lot wrong with it! If we were on pole by half a second there'd be nothing wrong with the car! But we're not, so there must be something wrong with it.

The F310B was a much better car than the F310, and Eddie Irvine revelled in its superior performance as he pushed Jacques Villeneuve all the way to the finish in Argentina.

'Clearly it needs more grip and consistency, all the normal things. There's nothing specifically wrong with it. The difficulty is that it's not

really my car and I don't understand it fully. So I'm trying to gain an understanding, and I'll introduce some of the ideas that I'm familiar with and see if they work on this package. Some do, some don't. It won't really be until 1998 that we have a car in whose design and devel-

opment Rory and I will have been involved.'

Nevertheless, the F310B succeeded beyond Schumacher's hopes on its debut in the Australian GP in Melbourne, where he finished second. Ever the pragmatist, he had outlined his expectations and strategy for the season before the start of the race.

'We won't be able to win races, in my view, not right from the beginning, anyhow,' he said. 'We should be able to get on the podium in the first couple of races. It is important to be there and to get the points. That would be good for us, because I want to score as many as possible at the beginning of the season, then give a challenge later on.' Brawn and Byrne soon had a beneficial effect, he said. 'They have already made a significant difference. The situation is much more calm.'

The better the performance of the team Jean Todt was building around him, the better defined the aspirations became. Back in 1996 there had been talk of an all-out push for the World Championship in 1997. Now, Brawn was again putting gentle brakes on. 'Obviously we want to win some races, because we want to do better than last year. But sometimes races disappear so brilliant in such conditions? How did he win the 1995 Belgian Grand Prix at Spa-Francorchamps, despite a period of running on slick tyres when the track was wet? Or the Spanish monsoon in 1996? The wet Belgian race again in 1997? Or the Silverstone deluge in 1998?

'What you need above everything else,' he says, 'is complete smoothness. You don't lock the brakes, you don't throw the car at the corner. You don't turn the steering wheel sharply. Everything you do must be done more gently than ever, with that smoothness that lets it change direction the way you want it to, not necessarily the way that the car wants to. It is like trying to coax a horse to jump a fence. You must be the one in control.'

At Spa in 1997, where the track was soaked just before the start by a sudden rainstorm, Schumacher dominated so much in the early stages, before the surface dried out, that he won by nearly half a minute. 'You know,' he said, 'when we were following the Safety Car which started the race, I looked up at the sky and felt better and better about my tyre choice. I started smiling, yes. I enjoy circumstances like that.

'Many people ask me why I do what I do. Well, a place like Spa gives me all the answers. It is a circuit on which you can express yourself. I look forward to coming here every year, wet or dry. Every time I go through the corner Eau Rouge, where it plunges downhill and then suddenly climbs again, it gives me a special feeling. A feeling like no other.

'When it is wet there you really have to push yourself. The car feels like it is on tiptoe, sliding, sliding. You seem to rush down all the time, then suddenly you are shooting towards the sky. You do not lift off. This is the ragged edge. You need commitment, of course, but more than anything you need absolute faith in yourself and in your machinery. This to me is what racing is all about.'

away from you for no good reason. At Benetton last year we had a couple of races which should have been in the bag, and they weren't. It's sometimes very difficult to do things well, so we've got to win some races. Michael's great, and he's capable of winning races he shouldn't win. And he doesn't throw away races that are in the bag.'

In the early part of the 1997 season McLaren rose to challenge Williams, with its powerful Mercedes engines and the driving force of David Coulthard and Mika Hakkinen. But once again the Ferrari was reliable. After finishing second in Australia Schumacher was fifth in Brazil and second again at Imola, before breaking through to another stunning wet-weather win at Monaco where he left his rivals floundering. Villeneuve recovered his momentum to win in Spain, but then Ferrari hit another purple patch as Schumacher lucked in at Montreal when Coulthard's clutch played up, then dominated at Magny-Cours. He was also walking the British GP before a wheel bearing failed. He was second at Hockenheim and fourth in Hungary, where the tortuous track proved less suited to the F310B's characteristics. Then Spa brought a fourth victory. This time Schumacher gambled on starting a wet race on intermediate tyres and when it was decided to make the start behind the safety car factors played into his capable hands. By the time the safety car let the racers get on with it, the track was drying, and in such changeable conditions the German has no peer. Nobody saw him again until he was waving to the crowd from the top step on the rostrum.

By this time he had already taken the lead in the World Championship, but now he stretched it to 12 points over Villeneuve. Ferrari was eight points ahead of Williams. But trouble was just around the corner. The car didn't work particularly well in either Monza or Austria, where Villeneuve won. And a first corner shunt with brother Ralf at the Nürburgring threw Schumacher behind the Canadian as they headed for the Japanese GP at Suzuka.

A so-called 'lightweight' F310B was ready just after mid-season, and by effectively moving the back of the seat forward a little Byrne had been able to accommodate another 10 litres of fuel, which would be crucial in opening up the size of the window available for refuelling strategy. This was an important car in another way, too, for it was a dry run for construction of the first pukka Maranello Ferrari for many seasons.

Chief mechanic Nigel Stepney, who

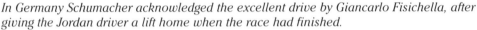

In Germany Schumacher acknowledged the excellent drive by Giancarlo Fisichella, after giving the Jordan driver a lift home when the race had finished.

transplanted himself from England and Team Lotus, and now loved every minute of living in Italy, summarised the team's progress at this point. 'We had just one or two mechanical failures, so it's been a good season in the respect that we've been able to deliver a car and finish races. That's good for us. Compared to before, it's a huge progression over what's been done in the past five years. It's just taken time, and we started from zero, really. It's happened because everything has stabilised and we've been able to work like a normal team should. When we were changing everybody each year, forget it. Now it's a nice atmosphere to work in.

'As for building the F310B, instead of having some bits shipped over everything was built for it at Maranello, where the basics existed. The drawing office now has more people in it, and that's another step in the right direction. It was all a good run for 1998.'

In Japan the Ferraris made best use of droopy front wings, incensing rivals who deemed them to contravene the spirit, though not the letter, of the regulations, and to enhance downforce by creating a degree of ground effect. And there Villeneuve stumbled, racing under appeal after being banned from the race for his fourth yellow flag contravention of the season. Here it was that Eddie Irvine came of age. He'd had a much better season than in 1996, finishing second in Argentina, right on

Red on the grid. Schumacher and his Ferrari engineers and mechanics prepare for the start of the Hungarian GP.

Villeneuve's tail, and third at Imola, Monaco and Magny-Cours. Now he led the race after passing the deliberately tardy Villeneuve, who was hoping his pace might slow Schumacher sufficiently so that slower rivals could take advantage and thus lose the German points. Later Eddie handed Michael the lead, then rode shotgun in his wake before dropping behind Frentzen to finish an honourable third. It was Todt using the tactic of team orders to perfection, although disgruntled rivals took a different view. 'It is thanks to Eddie that I have this win,' Schumacher said, but he added: 'but we have also made a big step forward in performance.'

With Villenueve duly kicked out of his eventual fifth place when his appeal was withdrawn, Schumacher was back in the championship lead, with 78 points to Villeneuve's 77. But Williams remained 18 points ahead in the Constructors' table. The stage was set for the great title shoot-out at the Grand Prix of Europe in Jerez, where a little extra stage management was suspected, as for the first time in history, three drivers – Villeneuve, Schumacher and Frentzen – tied for pole position with precisely the same lap time, measured in thousandths of a second.

Schumacher had carefully harvested tyres throughout qualifying, and rock-

Qualifying in Belgium was run on a dry track, but in the initially wet race Schumacher was again in a class of his own as he took his fourth victory at the Spa-Francorchamps circuit.

Arms raised aloft, Schumacher celebrates a stunning victory in Suzuka that was not only a triumph of team orders, but gave him fresh hope of winning the World Championship.

eted into the lead running on one of his fresh sets, as Villeneuve dropped momentarily behind Frentzen and Hakkinen while Coulthard, by prior arrangement, steered clear of the title fight. But after Schumacher and Villeneuve had made their first tyre stops on the abrasive little track in Spain's sherry region, Frentzen stayed out and now, like Irvine in Suzuka, he slowed the pace so that Villeneuve closed right up on Schumacher. They ran a second apart for many laps, until going into a sharp right-hander on the 48th lap, Villeneuve saw his chance and pounced down the inside of the Ferrari.

The French-Canadian came from a long way back and caught Schumacher completely by surprise. The corner was his, but after an initial attempt to block him, Schumacher then deliberately turned right, into the blue and white car, apparently intent on driving it off the road. It was the collision that everyone had predicted, pointing to the way in which Schumacher was deemed to have disposed of Damon Hill in Adelaide to win his first title back in 1994. But this time it was Schumacher who came off worse, the Ferrari sliding off on the outside of the corner. He was out of the race, and his stunned expression spoke volumes.

Like Hill's had been, Villeneuve's car was damaged, but he kept going. In the closing laps he 'thanked' the McLarens for their earlier courtesy by letting both pass him, and Mika Hakkinen scored an emotional first victory. However, Villeneuve's third place gave him enough points to overhaul Schumacher's World Championship lead, and as the storm broke over Schumacher's head, Jacques became the first ever French-Canadian to wear the crown.

Schumacher slunk away. Later he said, 'We feel we have enough reasons to be happy with the performance we have shown this year. As a team we have been, in my opinion, the number one team in Formula One and that is something that Ferrari can be very proud of.'

But Ferrari had lost a World Championship it could have won, at the last hurdle, and the world's press went into overdrive condemning Schumacher's dodgem car tactics.

The man who had been the idol of the Italian and German media, and the passionate fans in both countries, woke the following day to calls for Ferrari to sack him if he failed to apologise for the controversial clash.

The influential Italian daily paper, *Corriere dello Sport*, led with the front-page headline 'Schumacher – now apologise', while the *Gazzetta dello Sport* and *Tuttosport* both led with 'Schumi, what madness.'

For the first time in his career, the 28-year-old German was discovering

Prior to the fateful European GP at Jerez his stock with his fans had never been higher. But after his controversial collision with Villeneuve on the 48th lap, his comfortable world was momentarily to be turned upside down ...

how it felt to go from hero to zero. However much he tried to conceal his feelings, the furore in the Italian media came as a devastating blow to a driver used to adulation, and the F1 world began to ask whether the first serious cracks were appearing in armour which had been thought, prior to the GP of Europe, to be impenetrable.

Corriere chief Mario Sconcerti, in an editorial entitled 'Nobody has the right to want to win at all costs,' said that Schumacher should be sacked if he failed to apologise.

'I don't know what went through Schumacher's head the moment he turned his steering wheel sharply to the right to try and hit Villeneuve, nor what he felt when he sensed the world title slipping from his hand,' he said. 'I don't know what that flash of bitterness was, but it certainly wasn't sport … What happened was a dirty trick, an unworthy blow which in everyday life would have criminal consequences.'

Sconcerti, a passionate Ferrari fan, added: 'Today we call on Schumacher to apologise, not only to Villeneuve but also to all Ferrari people. This is no way to behave, this is no way to win, and we are not interested in victory at all costs.'

The *Gazetta*, which also headlined 'Villeneuve – a true champion', added to the attack on Schumacher with a column from chief Candido Cannavo.

'Let's disown the stain left by Schumacher's naïve and twisted attempt to force Villeneuve out, just as he was overtaking him with an impec-

Racing can be a family affair. At Silverstone in 1997 Michael shares a moment with Corinna and his brother Ralf.

Paul Stewart and Jean Todt are part of the group as Michael indulges his newfound interest in children.

cable, courageous and not reckless manoeuvre,' he said. 'It was an offensive scene for a duel which, whatever the outcome, would at least have maintained its dignity.'

In Germany Schumacher's popularity was also dented. Monday's *Bild* said, 'Schumacher himself was to blame for the crash,' and went on to pose the question: 'No question about it – Schumi wanted to push Villeneuve out. But Michael, why on earth did you do it?' *Frankfurter Allemagne* lamented the passing of Schumacher's 'nice boy next door' image, and attacked what it called his 'Wild West manners'. The *Saarbruecker Zeitung* declared: 'Schumacher's exit was the just punishment for an unfair attack.'

Villeneuve remained calm as he celebrated his achievement, but said: 'I knew Michael was capable of just trying to take me off and that's what he tried to do.' He didn't care whether Schumacher apologised or not.

Like Irvine, a man who speaks his mind, Villeneuve has since remained cold towards Schumacher, and even when the German made the unusual step of initiating some sort of *rapprochement* he maintained his stance. There is no love lost between them, and the coolness of their relationship is no product of F1's spin doctors. 'Why should I make anything up, when his behaviour on the track since Jerez gives the lie to his gesture?' Villeneuve asked.

It was a shattering end to Ferrari's season. It had come so close, yet had

Rainmaster: at Spa in 1997, Schumacher proved yet again that when the track is wet there is nobody remotely in his league.

stumbled again in controversial and embarrassing style that heaped worldwide disdain upon Maranello and its star driver. It was as if a carefully constructed house of cards had been blown down by one careless breath.

Surveying the crumbled ruin, Schumacher's manager, Willi Weber, wondered what he would do with 100,000 baseball caps he'd had printed with the premature legend: Michael Schumacher 1997 World Champion.

Chapter 5

Full gallop

The Australian Grand Prix, which kicked off the 1998 season in Melbourne, set the tone for what would become an increasingly bitter championship battle.

Ferrari had hidden away during the traditional round of pre-season testing, preferring to test at Fiorano and Mugello rather than joining others at Barcelona. As usual, stories were rife that the new car was in terrible trouble, and that it didn't work. Instead, the McLarens were the pacesetters, making full use of their winter switch from Goodyear tyres to Bridgestones. At that stage the Japanese tyres had a clear performance advantage, which Mika Hakkinen and David Coulthard were quick to exploit. Rival teams, especially those on Goodyears, were left to eat their dust. Against all expected form the narrower cars on the new grooved tyres which were now mandatory, proved little slower than their 1997 counterparts with their wide suspension and slick rubber. The new regulations had been expected to slow lap times by up to six seconds per lap, but as proof of the fertility of the technical minds in Formula One, Hakkinen's pole-position lap was less than seven tenths of a second slower than Villenueve's the previous year.

But even as the McLarens annexed the front row of the grid before racing away to unchallenged double triumph, the spectres of technical argument and industrial espionage haunted the paddock.

The argument was between McLaren and Ferrari, as the latter objected to McLaren's braking system. This enabled the drivers to favour one side of the car over the other to enhance its cornering performance by braking one rear wheel more than the other and thus turning it in more precisely. Ferrari and Tom Walkinshaw, whom John Barnard had joined in the Arrows team, solicited support for protest.

McLaren's pace in Melbourne for the opening race of the 1998 season stunned everyone, including Ferrari. For Schumacher the Australian GP provided a rare retirement, when his engine broke early on.

McLaren's Ron Dennis defended his system strongly, saying, 'It has been operative on our car since the middle of last year. The important thing to understand is that there is a very clear process laid down by the FIA to verify the legality of any element of design. It requires you to put in writing an explanation of any system and how it achieves a specific objective, and that is then carefully scrutinised by the technical delegate. When he is satis-

fied you get a sign-off. Our system was ultimately defined extremely accurately and we have in several instances had sign-off on the concept. As with anything else in a racing car, it is not the sole key. It is the sum of the total that gives you the performance. It contributes, yes. Is it a panacea? No.'

He shrugged off the threats. 'Any protest would have to be made in the normal way to the stewards who, I am sure, would call on their expert, the

The torture by McLaren continued in Brazil, where Schumacher had to be content with only fifth place as the Silver Arrows again hit the bullseye.

technical delegate. I can't see him having a different view to the one he has expressed in writing to us. It would be a pretty futile exercise.'

Then he moved into high gear, the inference of his ensuing comments aimed clearly at Ferrari. 'None of this has surprised us. It is clear that one team was the last out of the starting gate. Realisation has been followed by pure embarrassment, which has in turn been handled in an aggressive way. We know that up to four other teams are using a similar system.'

There had been another unsettling moment for McLaren during the weekend, when a photographer was thrown out of its garage on Friday when he was discovered taking spy shots of the cars.

'I am never surprised by anything in Formula One,' Dennis said. 'I think that different teams have different styles. Some teams have no style. On interrogation the photographer admitted to being the brother-in-law of one of the leading team's aerodynamicist.'

He cited other incidents of industrial espionage and indicated that he intended to take the matter up with the FIA. 'I think that, along with all Grand Prix teams, we are fiercely competitive. When any team has any sort of advantage you should make

It was third time lucky for Schumacher in the Argentinian Grand Prix, but would '98 also see him clinch the title for the third time?

strenuous efforts to understand why. But in the past there has been a code of conduct. There are some teams now, specifically one, which doesn't seem to have any code of conduct. So we have to take a more aggressive stance on their sort of behaviour. I think the most appropriate thing is to discuss it with the governing body to help us achieve what we think is a fair and balanced mechanism to protect our intellectual property. I don't think this is a sport where you reach for the law book for litigation at every opportunity. I'd rather avoid that at all cost. Hopefully a degree of embarrassment will arise from this situation.

If Michael leaves your team you've got your work cut out

'I can assure any team which wishes to challenge the validity of my statements, or feels sufficiently inclined to take any sort of steps to prove that what I have said is wrong, that they will be extremely embarrassed when we make material available.'

Dennis did little to discourage the view that Ferrari might be the team concerned, and when McLaren's protest was subsequently lodged – and upheld – following another McLaren 1–2 in Brazil, it set in train the bad feeling that was to characterise their fight for honours. At the same time, it set many observers pondering a tricky question. Was there one set of rules for

Ferrari, and another set for the rest? Neither Max Mosley nor Bernie Ecclestone, president and vice president of marketing of the FIA respectively, made the slightest secret of their desire to see Ferrari succeed. After all, apart from depriving Schumacher of his second place in the 1997 World Championship, the FIA had taken no serious action against him after Jerez, a deliberate offence for which most other drivers would have been banned for at least three races. It seemed incredible, unless cold logic dictated that the biggest box office draw had to appear, come what may. Then there was more than one incident in which Schumacher ignored a red flag in test sessions at Monza. Again, no penalties. Mosley had been quoted the previous year, during a tour of India, as saying that he would like to see the red cars win the title because it would be a nice change from Williams. At one stage Ecclestone told critics of Schumacher's driving to shut up, adding: 'Whingers are losers. Michael is just the sort of driver F1 needs.'

The precise truth of the situation was all but irrelevant, since Dennis so fervently believed the accusations he levelled in private.

Schumacher's engine had broken during his pursuit of the McLarens in

In mid-season Ferrari hit a purple patch. Hot on the heels of Schumacher's second victory, in Canada, he won the French GP too.

Overleaf: By 1998 Irvine was making a serious habit of finishing in the points. In Magny-Cours he backed Schuey brilliantly, to record Ferrari's 41st 1–2 finish.

Does Schumacher compare with Senna and Prost?

He is, pundits agree, one of the greatest drivers history has seen, and his 44th Grand Prix victory, at Sepang in 2000, moved him into second place ahead of Ayrton Senna and Nigel Mansell in the overall roll of winners. Only Alain Prost, with 51, has scored more triumphs. But how does Schumacher himself think he compares with Senna and Prost?

'I think we have two completely different characters, in Alain and Ayrton, and I would say that Alain Prost was always the thinking driver who – how can I say? – was not always looking so aggressive. Ayrton was really aggressive and you could always see that he was going to be really quick. Those were the two most outstanding differences I could see whenever I was racing closely with them.

'I think I was a mix between the two, but really I don't like to say because it is very difficult. I don't think, for example, that I brake any later than Ayrton, because there is a physical limit and you always try to be within this limit. But it depends how you go through the corner and out of the corner, whether you would put the car into a slide or whether you would keep it just within the limit. There are some issues where I give it a slide, and some where I don't. Alain, of course, would probably never give it a slide, whereas Ayrton probably always would.'

Would he think his style more similar to Ayrton's than to Alain's?

'Human beings are all different, and they approach things differently. To make comparisons, I think, would just be wrong. Much of it depends on the car, too. The only thing is you always have one driver who is the top. It looks like I'm the guy at the top, whereas before it used to be Alain Prost and then Ayrton Senna. But the way how you approach it is always different.'

Back in 1992 Nigel Mansell was adamant that Michael Schumacher was the man to watch for the future … His style, seen here in part at Hockenheim in 1997, places him right up there with the other modern greats, Ayrton Senna and Alain Prost.

Schumacher is known to prefer a car that turns in extremely well and is therefore prone to oversteer. This kind of car is more nervous to drive, and few other drivers like their cars set this way. 'I know that Jean Alesi's style is very similar and so was Nigel Mansell's', Gerhard Berger observed. 'I don't know how any of them can drive a car that way! I prefer some understeer. Even in the old days, with the Benetton with 1,300bhp from the BMW engine, I was only happy with an understeering car. Yes, I like to slide, but in low-speed corners. Jean, like Michael, likes to slide at 300kph! That's not for me! You can set your car up the same way, but that doesn't mean that you can automatically make that style work for you unless you like oversteer.'

Prost and Senna were rare drivers who could still be fast whether their cars understeered or oversteered, but where Senna was happy coping with oversteer at high speeds, Prost always preferred a degree of understeer.

Schumacher is from the same mould, but is he superior? It may still be too soon to say. Senna raced for just over ten seasons, Prost for 13, and each won three World Championships. Schumacher is now in his tenth full season (2001), and has won three titles so far. He has similar depth of experience to Senna and Prost, and has shown the same fortitude in adversity as Senna showed in 1993, or Prost in 1991. All three have been head and shoulders above their peers.

Australia, but he salvaged third place in Brazil. And there, indefatigable team-mate Eddie Irvine heaped fuel upon a fire he hoped would burn McLaren. Plain speaking had always been the cocky Ulsterman's stock-in-trade, and he saw no reason to stint himself on this occasion. 'Ferrari is gonna kick McLaren's butt,' he insisted. 'Ross knows good cars, and I know from driving this year's Ferrari in comparison to last year's that it is a much better car. When we get Goodyear's new wider front tyre, just watch. I can't handle understeer at all. I would run the car more on the nose than even Michael, to be honest. But he seems to be able to live with a bit of it.

Rivals were suggesting Ferrari had an illegal control system

'Michael is going to spank a few bottoms before long, to be honest with you. The tyres we had for Brazil were a lot more consistent than they were in Australia, but the newer still ones that we have coming for Argentina are going to be a big step. We've got a good compound with the Goodyears, but right now we don't have the same construction.'

He backed his argument by pointing out just how much fuel Schumacher had been carrying in Melbourne, on a one-stop policy, and how relatively little ground he had lost to them even so.

Within the sport Irvine is seen as a motormouth who likes nothing more than to be as controversial and outspoken as possible. But whenever he speaks of his illustrious team-mate he does so with unambiguous respect. It's an interesting side to the man. His is not the wide-eyed awe of some starstruck schoolkid trying to look hip, but the measured opinion of a man thoroughly qualified to express it.

'Put it this way,' he suggested. 'If Michael leaves your team, you know you've got your work cut out. Look at Benetton. Berger and Alesi were supposed superstars and had a far better car in 1996 and '97 than the one in which Michael won the championship in 1995, but what did they do with it?

'Michael is a lot younger than Senna was. He's not as flamboyant as Senna was. But for me Michael drives better than Senna did. Senna used to go round the corner blip-blip-blip on the throttle, and that's technically wrong. It had to be wrong! The laws of physics will say what the best line around a corner is. And blipping the throttle, going on and off the power, that isn't the quickest way.

'The thing is with Michael, the guy can get a corner perfect. So there's no point where you ever take time off him. With other drivers you'll take time off them under braking and they'd pull it back mid-corner, and whoever got the higher average would do the faster lap. It's a bit like Hakkinen and Coulthard, though they both drive very differently. Mika is a lot faster in high-speed corners. But Michael? He has no weak spots. He goes all the way in on the

After another win in the British GP, in further controversial fashion, Ferrari's form slumped. Even Schumacher couldn't make the F300 fly in Austria ...

brakes, and then he's just hard all the way on the throttle. There's no going round a corner blip-blip-blip.

'Everyone says that Hakkinen is quicker than Schumacher. Give me a break! I mean, Hakkinen sometimes gets outqualified by Coulthard. I saw them, Mika and Michael at Macau, don't forget, and Michael was just sensational at a time when nobody was taking Reynard seriously. Mika had a Ralt and Michael still beat him. When our car is right, it'll be no contest.'

Schumacher did not spare Goodyear, and his criticism reached

such heights at one stage that a public spat developed between Ferrari and Goodyear's representatives in Italy, who were subsequently forced to back down. It was an interesting index of the power of the Fiat-Ferrari combine.

Todt explained the situation calmly. 'It is just a fact. Michael said that the tyres were not good enough, and he was right. But it was nothing negative, it was just a statement. We know that Goodyear is trying hard, and they

Overleaf ... while Irvine had even bigger troubles in Hockenheim.

117

knew that the package that they were giving us was not good enough. So they are working hard on it, and that is normal. We know we have to improve the car as well. We hope that by improving the car and improving the tyres as well, we can fight to win races.'

Schumacher had said that he thought the majority of the deficit to McLaren lay in the tyres, but Todt declined to quantify the other areas. 'For sure the tyres are part of it,' he said. 'But quantifying these things is very difficult. How can I say that it is 70 per cent, 30 per cent? The best thing in this kind of situation is not to quantify but to work hard to try to catch up.'

The $64m question. Could Ferrari win the 1998 Championship?

The rumour mill suggested that Ferrari had had the chance to switch to Bridgestone for 1998, but that once McLaren had stolen a march and got there first there was no point, since McLaren's agreement provided for tyres to be designed specifically for the silver cars. At Goodyear Ferrari enjoyed a similar status, and the 1998 Goodyear became known as a 'Ferrari tyre', where in previous years they might have been known as 'Williams tyres'.

'We have a contract with Goodyear,' Todt explained, 'and even if lots of people say in F1 that you don't need to respect a contract, this is not my spirit. Whoever you are, if you have a contract you have a word. If I say something to you, but because I am F1 I know I will do the opposite thing, then there is no trust. I feel you need to have trust. The team has suppliers and sponsors, we have contracts. We have to respect that. On the one side I will say that I am happy to respect a contract. On the other we are not very happy not to have had a better package. But you have to be a good player. Goodyear are strong, they don't give up, so I hope that we can show finally that we were right to respect a contract. It would be justice and logic, and at the end of the day that is where the satisfaction comes.'

Certainly, Ferrari seemed to have caught and passed Williams, if you compared their respective performances at the end of 1997 and again after the early races of 1998, although McLaren has leap-frogged ahead of both of them. 'Ah,' Todt said quickly, 'but it is not McLaren alone! You ask about the tyres, and it is McLaren, Mercedes and Bridgestone, and we should never forget that. It is different. Last year all the top teams were on Goodyear, on the same kind of tyres. This year two of the best teams, one which is the quickest and most successful, are on a different type of tyre, so you have to take that into consideration.

'As for the situation with Williams, it isn't really progress because it's a new car and new regulations, so let's say we have probably been able to make a better car–engine package than they have been able to.'

But could Ferrari do that with McLaren, too?

It had a revised exhaust system in Argentina, together with the new engine that Schumacher successfully race debuted in Brazil. The precise significance of the former was lost on many, but insiders suggested it was a key element of the best engine management system in the business. It wouldn't be long before rivals were suggesting that Ferrari had an illegal traction control system, but what it actually had was a brilliantly sophisticated engine management system which used regulation of the fuel supply and the spark to create a fabulously usable power curve. It would be a critical ingredient in the team's performance as the season developed.

It transpired that Irvine was right, for although the new exhaust was not used in Argentina, Schumacher won the race after yet another controversial clash when he elbowed Coulthard out of the lead in a tight right-hand bend. Those who had called for him to be banned after Jerez immediately pointed to the return of his forceful tactics, and were outraged when no action was taken. For Ferrari it was a thoroughly satisfying result, with the added twist that as early as the third race it had ruined Dennis's aspirations to go one better than McLaren had in 1988, and to win every race.

A second at Imola was followed by a third in Barcelona as the McLarens again ran amok, and then another controversial – and unpunished – clash with Alexander Wurz at Monaco had put Schumacher out of the points. But he was about to hit a sudden roll that would have McLaren reeling. In Canada there were signs that Goodyear had recovered ground lost to Bridgestone, and Todt was cautiously optimistic prior to the race.

'It's difficult to know how much progress we have really made. We can be happy if we have progressed enough to be in front of the others. If we are behind, we cannot be happy. We have closed the gap slightly, yes, but we have to wait and see. Goodyear has been going big work as well, so the situation seems to have improved.'

The $64 million question. Did he still hold out hope at that time that Ferrari could win the World Championship in 1998? Todt responded with the caution of a man to whom such a reaction is ingrained after years of treatment at the hands of the Italian media. 'You know, to win the World Championship is difficult. It is even more difficult when you have a package as strong as the one we have in front of us. But we have to try. You don't always achieve what you want, but I can see what we are pretending to achieve.' He meant 'aspiring to achieve', one of the few times his English was less than perfect. In his heart he still believed that the great goal was still achievable, despite McLaren's apparent superiority.

'It is possible. We have been in worse situations. Very important is not to lose any more points to the others. Anyway, by the end of July we will know. We will have done eleven of the Grands Prix, so if something will happen, it will happen from now. Here in Canada, and at Magny-Cours and Silverstone.'

Three steps towards a stunning victory that threw the World Championship wide open as it moved beyond the mid-season point: Schumacher lines his F300 up in third place on the grid for the Hungarian GP …

And if Ferrari hadn't turned the corner by Silverstone, that would probably be it for the year? He smiled, a slow tolerant smile. 'Definitely.'

In Montreal Schumacher hounded Coulthard until the McLaren failed; in France he led Irvine home to Ferrari's 41st 1–2 and its first since 1990; and in Britain he drove a fabulous race in the rain to win for the first time on English soil. All of a sudden Hakkinen's massive points lead in the World Championship had been eroded – to two. The corner had been turned, and at maximum speed.

Yet none of the victories had come without controversy. In Canada he had emerged from a fast pit stop while the race was still under yellow caution flags, and as he pulled on to the racing line at the first corner had forced Heinz-Harald Frentzen off the road. He also missed the chicane at the end of the shoreline straight when overtaking a determined Damon Hill in his Jordan. He said that he hadn't seen Frentzen, and his critics believed his attack on Hill's tactics was designed to deflect criticism from his own. Again, McLaren wanted to know why he did not receive a mandatory 10-second stop-and-go penalty for missing the chicane.

Overleaf: After being told by Brawn at his second stop that he needs to make up 25 seconds in 19 laps on the McLarens, he drives at close to qualifying speed …

123

... Then makes a lightning third stop, emerging still in the lead to carry on for one of the greatest victories of his career.

In France Hakkinen had led the first start comfortably, but after Jos Verstappen had stalled his Stewart on the grid and the starting lights had momentarily malfunctioned, the race was red-flagged. At the restart Schumacher made another demon getaway and the result became a foregone conclusion. The grumbling that Ferrari was being favoured continued.

At Silverstone Hakkinen nursed a 38-second lead over Schumacher in changeable wet conditions, having made full use of his intermediate Bridgestone tyres' superiority on semi-dry track. He was still firmly in control when a downpour flooded the place and necessitated deployment of the safety car on the 43rd of 60 scheduled laps, despite a heart-stopping spin exiting the bridge corner which had sent the silver car spiralling across the grass before the Finn could bring it back under control. But the safety car closed everything up, and when the race was restarted six laps later it was not long before Schumacher began to hound Hakkinen, his Goodyears working at their best on the flooded road. When Hakkinen lost control of his car again, partly due to the damage inflicted earlier, Schumacher burst through into the lead and roared on to win.

He had, however, overtaken Alexander Wurz's Benetton under a yellow flag just prior to the appearance of the safety car, and as the race drew to its close it seemed that he

126

must stop for a 10-second penalty. Under the rules this could be added to his race time if the offence occurred within the final 12 laps, but clearly it had happened with 17 left. But the stewards did not advise Ferrari properly of the penalty, and it did not appear on the numerous television screens along the pit wall and in the press room. All Jean Todt received was a handwritten sheet of paper on which the precise clause of the regulations that applied was unclear. Moreover, the offence, which occurred at 3.15pm, was not officially recorded by the stewards until 3.39, and Ferrari was not informed of it until 3.43. Not only was this three minutes beyond the 25-minute time limit for such penalties, but Ferrari was told that the offence was an Article 57 violation which allowed for the penalty to be added to the driver's race time afterwards.

To cover himself, Todt had Schumacher brought in on his last lap, but due to the layout of the track he actually crossed the finish line before reaching the penalty spot, so effectively he had completed the race without stopping for a penalty which actually required him to undergo a stop-and-go penalty. Just to add to the confusion, Schumacher then rejoined and completed two further laps.

Further down the pit road, McLaren's personnel raised their arms in triumph,

believing Hakkinen had in fact won the race that he had hitherto dominated, but then a bemused Schumacher was told that he was the winner after all. Out came more bad feeling, and in went McLaren's protest, which the

This is the sort of pit lane support that it takes to run a top team. Now that McLaren has switched to West, the Ferrari crew is unique in wearing the red and white of Marlboro.

stewards later threw out. They chose as their grounds the fact that, since they had not recorded the penalty in the official way, and registered it on the television screen, it was null and void. Although McLaren's protest fee was returned, a fuming Dennis immediately registered his intention to go to the FIA Court of Appeal.

Thus, although 1998 was the year in which Ferrari's internal politics hit a record low, it was also the season in

which, externally, they scaled new heights.

Immediately after Silverstone, Schumacher and Irvine tested a longer wheelbase version of the F300 at Monza. 'I like it,' Schumacher said. 'On a circuit like this it's worth nearly half a second a lap.' And before the week was out Ferrari fired another salvo at McLaren by confirming that Schumacher had extended his agreement with the team. It had been due to expire at the end of 1999; now he would be staying until the end of the 2002 season. There is every possibility that the deal might well take the 29-year-old star to the end of his driving career.

To add to the confusion he completed two further laps

Gianni Agnelli, the 77-year-old patriarch of the Fiat empire, had already hinted strongly in recent weeks that Schumacher's contract would be extended, after speculation earlier in the season that he might squeeze out of it and switch to McLaren for 1999. A performance clause in his existing contract gave him an 'out' if he failed to finish in the top three in the 1998 World Championship. At the height of such talk McLaren had been winning everything, but the winning streak had been enough to convince Michael.

He is the essential ingredient for Ferrari's future. Since he was recruited

from Benetton the famous Scuderia had regenerated itself. In the four seasons since Alain Prost was sacked at the end of 1991, Ferrari had won but two races. Since the Schumacher era began in 1996, it had thus far won 12.

The new deal not only increased his annual salary from $30 million. It was said also to enhance the agreement wherein he could exploit Ferrari's name and famous Prancing Horse badge in his own merchandising. Both the Ferrari name and trademark ranked among the world's best brand names and logos. He had been granted a licence to print money. Such astonishing commercial freedom would have been unthinkable at McLaren.

In making the decision, Schumacher had, like Senna before him, weighed everything up to the smallest degree. And he liked what he saw. The technical situation had never been better. The annual budget was estimated by outsiders to be well in excess of $100 million. Ferrari, Michael Schumacher had concluded, was the best team in the business.

And what of the five-year plan Todt had outlined back in the middle of 1993? With a smile and a shrug, he says, 'Well, it has been tougher than I thought it would be. But believe me, it gives you better memories for the future. When it is tough, you remember. So I will have a lot of things to remember. And that makes victory sweeter. If I look back five years ago, we were dreaming to finish a race and score one point. Now when we finish second or third, it's national disaster!'

The politics within Ferrari seemed to be a ghost left in the past. 'You know, you need people to make politics, and I try to make other things. Everyone keeps busy, so we have less time to make politics …' Internally, that is. Outside the team itself, the politics swarmed around it with greater fervour than ever.

Besides Schumacher, Irvine's contribution to the success of Ferrari was often overlooked at that time, yet 1998 was his best season and he achieved some genuinely strong results. Fourth in Melbourne; third in Argentina and Imola, then again in Monaco and Canada, the latter after a drive from the back of the field; second in France; and third yet again in England.

'He is doing a better job this year because the car is better,' Todt affirmed. 'He is able to control the situation better. I would be happy to keep him with Michael next year, because I think we must concentrate on what we have. It is not good to change just for changing. They work well together.'

But it was Schumacher to whom the tribute for Ferrari's resurgence had to be paid. 'When you ask how much does a tyre contribute, how much does a chassis contribute, it is difficult,' Todt said. 'Michael is very strong and very good, but motor racing is a sport where you need to have a good car, a good package. Otherwise, look where Villeneuve is this year. Where is Hill this year? Because they are tired, they

By the time of the Italian GP in early September, the two Ferrari drivers were feeling sufficiently confident in Schumacher's title bid that they thought they would walk it.

are not motivated. So whoever you are, if you are the best, as Michael is, you need a good car if you want to be successful. If the gap is only three tenths of a second, you can cope with it. But if you are two seconds different, what can you do? So we must give him the best package and then it is up to him. But even he needs a good package, and we cannot expect him to do well and to win races if he doesn't have that good package.

The annual budget was well in excess of $100 million

'Never have I seen the slightest lack of motivation in him. But sometimes you are frustrated, which is normal, because you give so much of yourself. You start to be hungry and hungry to make it happen. Look at Monaco. He was not lacking motivation, but he was frustrated. He was trying to win or finish second, then he had to stop at the pit. But we had to carry on and he understood that. What would have happened if eight cars had retired in front of us, and we had missed one or two points? Look at last year. You never know. So as long as you are still racing to the chequered flag, things can happen. Never give up. If I ever feel that way, I will do another job.'

But Todt, like Michael Schumacher, has committed himself to Scuderia Ferrari Marlboro until well beyond 2000. And like Schumacher, he would

never lose motivation until the fight had been won. And when it had been, they would simply sit down and plan the next one.

After Silverstone Schumacher was only two points behind Hakkinen, 56 to 54, but in Austria and Germany the pendulum swung back to McLaren as Hakkinen took a brace of dominant victories ahead of Coulthard. But Hungary saw Ferrari and Schumacher pull off a stunning victory after changing their strategy partway through. They were helped when the front anti-rollbar worked loose on Hakkinen's car and he fell back, but Ross Brawn's strategic juggling and a fabulous drive in which Schumacher did as Ross instructed and opened a 19-second lead in 25 laps, were crucial factors.

Then came Spa, the season's most controversial race, and Michael's controversial incident while lapping Coulthard. This was the race in which a spin by Coulthard exiting the La Source hairpin at the start triggered off a multiple shunt which led to the race being stopped. Whether Irvine tapped the Scot into his rotation was never determined conclusively enough to apportion blame. Then Hakkinen made an overly cautious restart, and in trying to avoid Damon Hill's Jordan (which would go on to win), he was tapped gently into a spin by Schumacher. The McLaren was then rendered *hors de combat* by Johnny Herbert's Sauber, and suddenly Ferrari was looking very good. It looked better still when Michael passed Hill for the lead with a stunning move going down to the Bus Stop chicane, flat out in the rain. But then came the moment when he collided with Coulthard as the Scot slowed to let him by as he was being lapped. Michael had a huge lead and, for the first time, was on target to take the championship initiative, until he lost his right front wheel as the rear end of the McLaren suddenly loomed at him out of the gloom. Angrily three-wheeling home, he gave full vent to his spleen on Coulthard, demanding to know if he was trying to kill him. Most observers took the view that Michael had made an error, and that Coulthard had done nothing deliberate, and later Schumacher would calm down when discussing the controversy.

'It was not so much what David did that lap,' Luca di Montezemolo said, 'as what he had done the lap before, when he closed the door on Michael and held him up for the full lap. Spa is seven kilometres long, don't forget, one of the longest tracks on the calendar. That was not acceptable.'

Thus both championship contenders left Belgium empty-handed, but Ferrari exacted revenge at Monza, where everyone had expected McLaren to dominate. Both McLaren drivers made fabulous starts, but Coulthard blew up and Schumacher caught and passed Hakkinen, who later dropped back to sixth with serious braking problems. It had been a catastrophic race for McLaren, and suddenly the heavy betting was on Schumacher riding to his third World Championship on Ferrari's regained

Michael Schumacher and Ross Brawn: one of the great driver/engineer relationships of modern times.

tide of momentum. There were, after all, only two races left. While McLaren still had the best car, Ferrari had the best driver, the best tyres, the best strategy and, perhaps most important of all, the best reliability.

He had run over debris, and Ferrari's great quest was over

At the Nürburgring Schumacher and Ferrari dominated qualifying for the GP of Luxembourg, and to McLaren's dismay Irvine was also on the front row. But after Schumacher had sprinted into the lead and Hakkinen had scrambled past Irvine, whose brakes were playing up, and went on to pass Michael during their first pit stops, and do to him what he usually did to others by using fast laps while his rival was refuelling, to snatch the lead. After that the Finn kept everything under control to take a stunning seventh triumph of the season, leaving Schumacher looking shellshocked. In the immediate aftermath, even Michael began to make tentative concessions which suggested that he thought his championship chance was slipping away. The scene was set for the great showdown at Suzuka.

Ferrari tested for 17 of the 32 days between the races. 'I don't know why,' Michael said one day after testing at Mugello, 'but I have this deep feeling that I am going to win a third title.'

In Suzuka Schumacher took pole

from Hakkinen, and the two shook hands on the grid. Earlier, di Montezemolo had sat down for an hour with Ron Dennis. 'I am here because first of all I wanted to support the team,' he said. 'But also, win or lose, I wanted personally to shake his hand. I think it is important for the name of sport that we are seen to be talking.'

Multiple scenarios had been propounded but, ironically, everyone overlooked the possibility that Schumacher might stall at the start. First Jarno Trulli did so in his Prost and was sent to the back. Then Michael did the same. The clutch had overheated and dragged during the delay before the red start lights went out, possibly because he had already tried two racing starts in the warm-up laps.

Hakkinen surged confidently into the lead ahead of Irvine, yet by the end of the first lap Michael had gone from 21st to 12th. Then he got bogged down behind Hill and Villeneuve, fighting over fifth place. Hakkinen went away at two seconds a lap, but Michael was up to third, charging, by lap 30. One lap later, Tuero and Takagi tangled in the chicane, and suddenly it was all over. As Schumacher completed his 31st lap the right rear Goodyear tyre exploded just as Nigel Mansell's had in Adelaide in 1986. He had run over debris, and Ferrari's great quest was over.

He described how much he had enjoyed his adrenalin charge. 'The first couple of laps were good fun. All the other drivers were very fair and did not try to make life difficult. But I never expected a rear tyre to explode, because actually I was worried about the fronts as I had flat-spotted one and had a lot of vibration. But I don't feel too disappointed. I think we did not lose this championship today, but in the early stages of the season when we were too far behind.'

'I am extremely proud of Ferrari and what it has achieved,' said di Montezemolo. 'We have nothing to be ashamed of. Today's race was a roulette; 1998 is now over. It is the end of one dream, but the beginning of another. McLaren has done a fantastic job, so *chapeau* to them. But we will be back next year, and we will win.'

After one of the best seasons in recent memory Ferrari had lost, but it had done so with a dignity that befitted the sport's most charismatic team.

Chapter 6

Qualified success

What would have happened had Michael Schumacher not crashed on the first lap of the 1999 British Grand Prix at Silverstone in July?

It was a question that would haunt Ferrari for the remainder of a year in which, even with its German star sidelined through what some saw as his own impetuosity, it would be crowned as World Champion Constructor and would nevertheless come tantalisingly

Eddie Irvine's Great Day: the Ulsterman heads for his first Grand Prix victory under the Melbourne sun, and takes the lead in the World Championship.

close to the World Championship for Drivers.

Yet again the season had begun with the usual mix of platitudes and lofty aspirations outlined at the team's new car launch in Maranello. This time the team would begin well and would have a car capable of challenging McLaren from the outset, Luca di Montezemolo suggested, but this time the facts bore him out. Ferrari won the Australian GP, which as usual kicked off the season in Melbourne.

But it was not Michael Schumacher at the wheel of the victorious F399. The victory Down Under was the first for the faithful Eddie Irvine. The Ulsterman qualified sixth fastest, but was handed a bonus by his old Jordan partner Rubens Barrichello who had to surrender his fourth slot when his new Stewart-Ford caught fire on the grid. This was good news for Ferrari, as when Michael encountered a problem on the formation lap with his car's neutral reset button and lost his third place, he was obliged to start at the back.

The two McLarens took off in the lead, with Irvine taking an immediate third. When Coulthard's hydraulics went awry on the 14th lap, Eddie moved up to second and when Hakkinen's silver arrow faltered four laps later, he was leading. Michael, meanwhile, had recovered to fourth place with 35 laps remaining, and as the safety car was deployed when Alex Zanardi shunted his Williams heavily, the German's prospects were looking good. But on the 27th lap his hopes took a dive when his gear selection problems returned, the F399 tending to select neutral when cornering. A change of steering wheel eventually cured the problem, but by then he was way out of contention.

It was thus left to Eddie to uphold Ferrari honour, and this he did, resist-

Brotherly love: an ecstatic Irvine embraces sister Sonia in the moment of triumph.

ing a challenge from Heinz-Harald Frentzen's Jordan to win by one second.

The early races suggested that McLaren's ploy of optimising its new MP4/14 performance as a priority over its reliability was a double-edged sword. The silver arrows were still the fastest cars, both in qualifying and in race trim. But Hakkinen and Coulthard both retired in Australia, and the Scot failed to finish again in Brazil, too. Hakkinen won there, however, as Irvine backed his Australian result with fifth place and Schumacher kicked off his points score with second.

Schumacher's arrival each day was met with muted enthusiasm

If you need a definition of a driver who makes the tifosi happy, it is the Ferrari pilot who has just secured a good result. On that basis, both Schumacher and Eddie Irvine's stock was very high in Italian circles early in 1999. There was an ironical amusement in Schumacher's case, for when it was announced at Monza in 1995 that the tifosi's beloved Jean Alesi and Gerhard Berger were leaving, to be replaced by Schumacher and Irvine for 1996, the news was met with derision in the Italian media. Whenever Alesi went to the paddock gates at the famous autodromo to sign autographs, he was mobbed. Schumacher's arrival each day was met with muted enthusi-

asm. Some who jammed the gates cheered when he made an appearance, but it was hardly the rapturous screaming with which every glimpse of Berger or Alesi was greeted. Nor, by Imola 1996, were there anything like as many banners for the German as for the men, particularly Gerhard, whom he had replaced. But pole position for that San Marino GP went a long way towards cementing the relationship, and second place, followed later in the season by three hard-fought victories, began to confirm Schumacher as another favourite. Now that he had actually donned the red overalls – and won for Ferrari – the tifosi had come to adore him. But then came Jerez in 1997, and a fall from favour. The vitriol served up by the Italian media, and, it seemed, by the tifosi, left the German deeply shocked, no matter what external face he liked to present to the world.

While 1998 had been his year of penitence and redemption, by 1999 he was again back in favour. Victory at Imola over a frustrated Coulthard and a mechanically unreliable Hakkinen did much to boost his stock. He followed it with another excellent victory around the streets of Monte Carlo, and a damage-limiting third behind the fleet McLarens in the Spanish GP at Barcelona.

The Circuit di Catalunya is one of those technical venues that highlights a car's true capabilities, since it combines a variety of corners with its long, long pit straight. The two opposite sides of the aerodynamic coin are thus thrown into sharp focus for all to see: grip versus drag. And as usual,

Fifth place in Brazil the next time out was sufficient to retain the championship lead for Irvine.

McLaren had the best compromise and the fastest cars. The Ferraris struggled in their wake. But the Ferraris were proving to be bulletproof after Schumacher's surprise problem in Melbourne. While Coulthard had only two finishes to he credit, Irvine had retired only at Imola, when he slid off the road on his own oil after it was his turn to suffer an engine failure. Incredibly, it would prove to be his sole retirement of the season, and only once more would he fail to score points.

Hakkinen won again in Canada, where Michael somewhat uncharacteristically blotted his work by shunting into the wall exiting the final corner. It was a very public mistake. The German had taken pole position and had aggressively and ruthlessly chopped across Hakkinen at the start to frustrate any ambition the Finn had of grabbing an early lead. It was a tactic that he would employ increasingly the

following season. But then the race was stopped when Jarno Trulli and Jean Alesi came together in the first corner.

The safety car was deployed until the second lap, whereupon Schumacher resumed the lead with Hakkinen hot on his heels. Three laps later the safety car was out again, this time after Ricardo Zonta had hit the wall opposite the pits, after fudging his exit from the last corner. This is a tricky and tight right/left flick at the end of a long straight, and obliges drivers to brake hard before making a definite right turn followed immediately by a left turn. The danger lies either in braking too late or in carrying a fraction too much speed through the corner and then sliding wide in to the inviting wall. The young Brazilian would not be the only driver to make an error there.

When racing resumed again it was clear that Hakkinen could stay with Schumacher, but the Ferrari driver had the advantage on a circuit on which overtaking is notoriously difficult. Better still for Ferrari, Irvine was holding third place, albeit five and a half seconds adrift.

In an instant Ferrari's race turned from promise to nightmare

Damon Hill became the second victim of the final corner, crashing hard on the 15th lap, but Schumacher continued now to ease away from Hakkinen. After 28 laps he had carefully constructed a lead of just under five seconds, but then disaster struck. This time it was Michael who fell foul of the slippery surface in the final corner, as he came up to complete his 30th lap. In an instant Ferrari's race turned from promise to nightmare as the red car understeered too far and crumpled itself helplessly into the unyielding concrete. No sooner had the Ferrari been craned away than Jacques Villeneuve did exactly the same thing, but that was no consolation to Schumacher as he strode away, his mood written across his expressive face for all too see. It had been a very public mistake, and had cost him his lead in the World Championship. Instead of extending that to 10 points, he was now four behind the Finn.

Hakkinen gratefully accepted the victory that had just been handed to him, while Irvine remained third after being outfumbled in the pit stops by Giancarlo Fisichella in a Benetton. Even at this stage it was clear that, while the Ulsterman was keeping his challenge alive, Ferrari only had eyes for Schumacher. Circumstance would soon change all that, however.

Just as McLaren liked Barcelona, so it liked Magny-Cours. The ultra-smooth French track really suited the MP4/14s, and practice indicated that Ferrari would struggle in comparison. But in qualifying the weather did its best to reshuffle the pack, giving Rubens Barrichello pole position from Jean Alesi, in Stewart and Sauber retrospectively, as they were smart enough to venture out before a vast overhead cloud deposited its contents all over the race track. Of the topline team drivers, Coulthard was best in fourth place on the grid, with Schumacher sixth, Hakkinen only 14th and Irvine, the last official qualifier, in 17th. Because of the conditions, Hill, de la Rosa, Takagi, Badoer and Gene did not circulate within the 107 per cent rule, but were allowed to start.

On paper, Schumacher had the best chance, given his flair in the rain and the conditions on raceday, but as Heinz-Harald Frentzen scored a remarkable victory over Hakkinen following some inspired strategic thinking, Schumacher could only manage fifth place. What's more, Ferrari actually permitted Michael's brother Ralf to get away with fourth place, rather than allowing Irvine to move ahead of his team leader to challenge the Williams. Had the

As always, Eddie knew how to amuse himself in Sao Paulo.

Irvine always looked the part, and thoroughly enjoyed his moment in the spotlight.

Ulsterman been allowed to vault ahead of one German, and successfully challenged the other, he would have finished the title chase at least on equal points with Hakkinen.

But that was all in the future that afternoon, when Schumacher was still the team's major star.

The race had started going awry for most when the safety car was deployed at the end of the 22nd lap, as the rain that had affected qualifying and which had been expected all morning

returned in time to render the track a skating rink. Schumacher had taken sixth off the line, but Irvine admitted that he was still in neutral and lost time selecting first gear. Ahead, Coulthard lost no time grabbing the lead from Barrichello, as Hakkinen carved towards the front. But Schumacher seemed subdued, by the standards observers had come to expect of him in such conditions.

Irvine, meanwhile, had deliberately taken things easy in the opening laps, but began gradually moving up until he was ninth just when the rain arrived. He immediately radioed his crew that he would make a pit stop, but the stop proved disastrous. The mechanics were busy readying him another set of dry weather grooved tyres, not a set of wets. Instead of being stationary in the pits for around 10 seconds, he was there for almost 43 and plummeted down the order.

The safety car stayed out until the 35th lap, whereupon Barrichello resumed the lead (Coulthard long having retired with electrical failure), challenged by Hakkinen. But then the Finn spun briefly, allowing Michael through to challenge the man who was already being tipped as his team-mate for 2000. He moved ahead on lap 44, and then began to pull away. By lap 50 he had an advantage of just under nine seconds, and things were finally looking good for Ferrari. But in the cockpit Schumacher was struggling to select first and second gears, and he pitted on the 54th lap for a replacement steering wheel in case the problem lay with its selector paddles. It was the same problem that had hurt him in Melbourne.

Now he was fourth, behind Barrichello, Hakkinen and Frentzen. Worse still, brother Ralf came pushing through into fourth place, as Michael struggled on the drying track. Irvine was clearly quicker, but team orders obliged him to fume quietly in his 'boss's' wake.

'Basically we made too many mistakes in the difficult conditions,' Irvine admitted, while refraining from venting his obvious frustration. 'You know,' he added, 'we had a better car today, but we just failed to capitalise on it ...'

But if Eddie thought that a thoroughly frustrating day had given him the pit stop from hell, worse was waiting for him at the new Nürburgring ...

Morale was low in the Ferrari camp long before the British GP, but Schumacher boosted the mood by

qualifying behind only Hakkinen with Irvine similarly close to third-placed Coulthard. The red cars were competitive again, but there was much work to do. Two poor races had eroded the advantage, and now Hakkinen headed the points table with 40 to Michael's 32 and Eddie's 26. All was not lost by any means, but Schumacher knew he had to turn the tide if he was to retain realistic hopes of beating Hakkinen.

Close friends suggest that he had been increasingly irked by Irvine's insouciant pace in recent races, while one who had invited the German to dine with him and other friends on the Saturday evening found him quiet and withdrawn.

The following day he made a poor start as the British GP got underway. Hakkinen and Coulthard led off the

Brothers in arms: Michael and Ralf Schumacher were never far apart, even at race meetings.

line in their McLaren-Mercedes, but Schumacher had too much wheelspin and was immediately overtaken by Irvine. But Eddie made a mistake at Becketts, where a fast-recovering Michael reeled him in, then the German seemed irate and unsettled as they headed through Chapel and on to the fast Hangar Straight, as Irvine steadfastly refused to cede third place on the run down to Stowe.

The two Ferraris barrelled down the straight still fighting one another. Ahead of them, and directly behind, however, the McLaren and Jordan drivers already knew that the race had been red flagged. Back on the grid, Jacques Villeneuve's BAR and Alex Zanardi's Williams had both stalled. Rather than try to move the cars in the limited time available, the race officials red flagged the event.

Neither of the Ferrari pilots was aware of this in their private duel. Going into Stowe Schumacher tried to dive inside Irvine, on a tight line that many felt would not in any case have allowed him to make the turn without running very wide on the exit. But there was another factor at work. It would transpire that a rear brake bleed nipple on the Ferrari was loose and therefore leaking, and with brakes only on the front wheels the German suddenly found himself in serious trouble. The red car failed to make the corner and skipped precariously over the gravel run-off as if it were tarmac, and then embedded itself nose-first

Double top in Monaco was more than just cause for Schumacher and Irvine to start celebrating in style.

into the two-layer tyre wall. The front end of the monocoque cracked and broke away in the heavy impact, and Schumacher sustained double fractures in his right leg. His World Championship challenge was over for another year.

'The most spectacular accidents are the ones you don't have to worry about'

Peter Wright, the FIA's technical delegate, later calculated that Schumacher was still travelling at 120mph (193kph) after braking heavily on the tarmac, and left the track at that speed. He scrubbed some speed off as he bounced over the gravel, although FIA president Max Mosley later expressed the view that he might have lost more if he had had the presence of mind to turn the steering wheel. Instead, Schumacher kept the wheels pointing straight ahead as he crashed heavily through the tyre barrier and used up most of the crushability that was designed into the Ferrari's nose. He was thus fortunate that the chassis then failed, giving him a critical further stage of mechanical deformability before he himself became damaged.

'Basically, a front wheel came round and hit the side of the monocoque, which buckled,' Wright explained. 'But that structural collapse gave him another metre for deceleration, which probably saved him. He was going a bit quick for the barrier.'

There were plenty of tyres stacked on the outside of the gravel trap at Stowe, but they had not been tied together with conveyor belting because nobody had been expected to go off the track there. 'It's exactly that case, where you don't expect something to happen at a specific point,' Wright admits, 'and when it does your reaction is, "Oh, shit!"'

It is always very easy in the aftermath of such serious accidents to ask why nobody had thought that what actually happened might really happen. But often the answer is more complex than the question. Wright was tasked with writing a report on the accident for Mosley, and explained his findings. 'I made a plot of what the car did, particularly through the gravel bed, and subsequently we released the numbers to the press. That just damped down the crap that we could see was beginning to build up.

'The gravel bed slowed the car as well as the car was slowing down on the track. The car was down to 1.3g when it left the circuit, and had only got front brakes. The front tyres were down to the canvas. It was categorically said by Ferrari that there was a rear brake failure. I saw my trace and Ferrari's trace, and there was nothing that contradicts that.

'The most spectacular accidents are the ones you don't have to worry about. The worst ones are when the car goes in and appears to be hardly damaged. When Schumacher went into the tyres you could tell it was quite bad. Okay, he was in the tyre barrier, which made a big difference, but it's the ones where not a lot of stuff appears to have been knocked off the car that you worry about. He went in at 106–109kph [66–68mph], having left the track at 193kph [120mph] and decelerated across the gravel at an average of 1.1g, which was about what he would have done if he had stayed on the track.'

None of this was of much comfort to Schumacher or Ferrari. Jean Todt went with the German to Northampton General Hospital, where it became clear that Michael would be out of action for some time. He had a double fracture below his right knee, and underwent a 90-minute operation. One broken bone was pinned, the steel remaining in Michael's leg until the end of the 2000 season.

So had Schumacher just got himself into a snit with Irvine and paid a heavy price for his impetuous lunge up the inside going to Stowe? Or did the leaking brake bleed nipple really hurt his chances of making the corner? Wright certainly concurred with the latter suggestion, but when it was later put to Irvine that he had got Michael rattled, the Ulsterman merely smiled and offered the 'You may think that but I could not possibly comment,' sort of response.

In the hoopla that followed Schumacher's shunt speculation knew no bounds. Would he quit altogether, having had those split seconds in which to watch the wall approaching at high speed? Would he have lost that vital last ounce of nerve, now that he had broken bones in a racing car? Would he be the same driver afterwards?

On more than one occasion in early 1999 Schumacher and Irvine enjoyed the spoils of victory.

'I know I'm going to be out of action for two to three months,' Schumacher admitted, 'and I realise that I have absolutely no chance of the championship this year. But I am confident that I'll be back driving a Ferrari in Formula One before the end of the season.'

'I realise that I have no chance of the Championship this year'

In the meantime, Ferrari had more than one dilemma. First, Todt had to find a replacement driver for the one whom everybody in F1 believed was irreplaceable. Secondly, there was the question of Ferrari's continuing challenge for the World Championship for Drivers. Irvine was still in the hunt, but would Ferrari really put all its efforts behind him? Or did the Scuderia really want to wait until Schumacher was fit again, to try to make him its first champion since Jody Scheckter, when the 2000 season got started? There was as much speculation over the team's intentions as there was over the true cause of Schumacher's accident, but though it made news headlines to suggest that Ferrari would really 'throw' its chances, to let Michael be the breakthrough champion as and when, it really made little or no sense for a team which had invested so much in the chase willingly to do less than its best to secure the title.

Whatever, Irvine would do little to help make any decision there might have been an easy one. Although Coulthard won the British GP after a wheel fell off Hakkinen's wagon, Irv the Swerve followed him home (actually being accused of losing the race himself by slightly over-shooting his pit during his refuelling stop) to maintain joint second place only 10 points behind Hakkinen. The chase was far from over.

Then came Spielberg and Hockenheim. Todt had sensibly appointed the former Lotus, Tyrrell and Arrows star Mika Salo to stand in for Schumacher (although that would later lead to a law suit between Salo's management and BAR, which had used him for a few races earlier in the season when Ricardo Zonta was indisposed). Yet again the McLarens annexed the front row, but Irvine was third fastest even if he wasn't happy about a time one second shy of Hakkinen. 'We underperformed,' he growled, irritated by a brake problem.

Irvine insisted that the race would be a different matter, and circumstances proved him right. On the first lap Coulthard pulled a move on Hakkinen for the lead, but it didn't come off. Instead, he ended up beaching his team-mate. That left the Scot to lead from Barrichello, whose continuing strong form in the Stewart-Ford was continuing to attract Todt's eye. Irvine settled into third straight away, but further back Salo smudged his work by nerfing Johnny Herbert off on the first lap and damaging his Ferrari's front wing. The Finn would finish a disappointing ninth, but his time would come …

148

Ferrari's bubble burst at Silverstone. As Schumacher hit the tyre wall at Stowe and was then stretchered away to Northampton General Hospital with a broken right leg, the Scuderia's title hopes appeared to have gone with him.

Meanwhile, Irvine took advantage of Barrichello's fuel stop on the 38th lap to move into second place, his deliberate strategy of taking things relatively easy in the opening stages beginning to pay off. The big dividend came just two laps prior to the Brazilian pitting, when Alex Zanardi's Williams rolled slowly through the last corner, out of fuel. Coulthard was momentarily baulked, just as Irvine was really starting to motor in the Ferrari. He'd saved fuel early in the race, and now he could afford to push really hard.

Coulthard pitted on the 39th lap, promoting Irvine to the lead. But such was the Ulsterman's pace that when he made his own pit call five laps later he was able to emerge with a lead still a

hair under two seconds over the McLaren. With Hakkinen staging a blistering recovery in third place the scene was set for a nail-biting finish. Lap by lap Coulthard got closer to Irvine, but the Ferrari driver was not putting a wheel wrong in quite the most convincing performance of his career. He was the team leader, and he was driving like one. Coulthard could get close, but it became clear that Irvine was not going to crack under the pressure.

Towards the end puffs of smoke were visible in the red car's wake. Afterwards Eddie provided an amusing explanation. 'They were probably coming from my brain, I was so overloaded,' he said. The Ferrari had been a handful on its second set of

The amiable Finn, Mika Salo, was the man chosen to support Irvine, while Schumacher recovered. Here he explains Ferrari's steering wheel to rally champion Tommi Mäkinen.

Bridgestone tyres, and the brakes had been unsatisfactory, so he had been struggling. 'In the end I just had to forget about the problems and just start pushing to stay ahead of DC,' he added.

Suddenly both championships were firmly back within Ferrari's reach. Coulthard's unintentional attack on Hakkinen, and his inability to pass Irvine, meant the Finn now had only two points more than Irvine as they headed to Germany.

At Hockenheim, Mika Salo would drive the race of his life. Now much more familiar with his new mount, he outqualified Irvine, took on and beat Coulthard with almost disdainful ease, and took the lead on the 25th lap when Hakkinen, who had opened a comfort-able advantage over everyone, suffered a sudden rear tyre blow out and departed the race at high speed. But Salo had not been employed to star for Ferrari; his job was to score points and to help Irvine all he could. Within a lap of taking over at the front, he was obliged to let his team-mate by. Without that, he would deservedly have won his first GP.

Irvine was in trouble throughout qualifying, prompting critics to suggest that he could not set-up his Ferrari without Schumacher there to provide the guidelines. This was unfair criticism, but Irv's failure to do better than fifth on the grid for what would be a crucial race did not help his cause. He slid off the road entering the stadium during his first attempt, and then went

Former Ferrari racer, Stefan Johansson, paid a trip to the Ferrari garage, where he was entertained by Salo and Irvine.

down the wrong road on set-up when trying to salvage the afternoon. Traffic on his final run left him only fifth, and busily explaining how his best sector times would have put him on the front row. Schumacher, his detractors said, would have done just that.

As the second McLaren moved away Irvine began to move up

Initially he ran only sixth as Salo pounced into second place on the opening lap and fended off Coulthard's persistent attentions. Then the Scot damaged a nose wing after getting too close to a door-closing Salo in one of the chicanes. As the second McLaren dropped away Irvine began to move up. Barrichello vacated fifth place after six laps, then Coulthard fell back, leaving Eddie to chase after Heinz-Harald Frentzen's Jordan. He took over third place when the German stopped for fuel on the 21st lap, and kept ahead of the yellow car after stopping himself a lap later. Ferrari's excellent pit work got Salo out in third place next time around, and once interloper Ralf Schumacher had finally made his stop after rising as high as second while others made theirs sooner, Hakkinen was left leading from Salo and Irvine. Then the Finn pitted on his 24th lap, dropping to fourth in a closely fought encounter. He had just passed Frentzen, in readiness for the long haul after the Ferraris when his left rear tyre

exploded going into the stadium. As one Finn departed, however, so the other was left savouring leading a GP for the first time. But when the call to let Irvine pass came, Mika responded instantly, his selflessness earning him much praise.

It was not the way in which Eddie Irvine would have wanted to win the third GP of his career and the second in succession, but a win is a win. He talked of the McLarens 'shooting themselves in the foot', and he paid full tribute to Salo as Ferrari celebrated a 16-point haul on a day when McLaren scored only two for the delayed Coulthard's fifth place. As Irvine regained the championship lead for the first time since Brazil in March – and a lead of eight points, at that – those who had harped on about his lack of qualifying speed now began producing who-needs-Schumacher stories. But the intelligent interpreters of F1 fortunes know that Ferrari had been lucky in the last two races, and that McLaren still had the quicker car. It just seemed as if the British team was looking for ways not to win the title.

Behind the scenes other things were very clear; despite his latest victories Irvine would not be staying at Ferrari beyond the end of the season. He played a brilliant tactical game, breaking the news as if it was his decision, where others later suggested it had been Ferrari's. For no short while it was even possible that he would race alongside Hakkinen at McLaren, as Adrian Newey and Martin Whitmarsh were trying to erase Ron Dennis's reservations about a maverick who would never seem likely to settle into

McLaren's corporate mould. But even before his latest triumph Irvine knew another door had closed; on raceday morning Dennis finally confirmed that Coulthard would be staying to partner the Finn. Irvine looked instead to Jaguar's plan to create its own identity out of the competitive Stewart-Ford team that Ford had purchased in June.

In the immediate aftermath of Hockenheim, Jean Todt and the team at Ferrari were vilified by the Italian media for spending so much money on Schumacher when Salo could appar-

Thanks Mika! On the podium at Hockenheim, Irvine expresses his gratitude to Salo, after the Finn obeyed team orders and had handed the Ulsterman what should have been his own first GP victory.

ently do a similar job for a fraction of the German's inflated fee. But Hungary brought Salo down to earth with a bump. Irvine lost out by only a tenth of a second to Hakkinen for pole position, but Mika could only qualify 18th, two seconds off his team leader. Clearly something was awry, and while Salo maintained a diplomatic silence and spoke of his car being 'difficult', others suggested that he was obliged to qualify with a high fuel load, a tired engine and old tyres. Whatever, the Italian media quickly lost interest in him as the new, cut-price Messiah.

Clearly something was awry and Salo maintained a diplomatic silence

Despite starting on the dirty side of the grid, Irvine maintained second place for the first 29 laps, until his first fuel stop. But 15 laps from the end he ran wide on a corner at the back of the circuit, and Coulthard gratefully snatched the place away. Like Magny-Cours it was an expensive mistake, only this time it was the driver's and not the team's. With Salo an undistinguished 12th, Ferrari left Hungary with a two-point lead over Hakkinen in the Driver's Championship, and four over McLaren in the Constructors'. There was no room for complacency.

There was a ray of hope for Ferrari in Belgium, when Irvine took a front row grid position alongside Hakkinen, but again Salo disappointed with only 18th

slot. The race disappointed, even though Coulthard asserted himself over Hakkinen and refused to assist the Finn's quest for maximum points. But with Frentzen also heading the Ferrari leader home, fourth place was a poor show. Now Hakkinen had 60 points, Eddie 59. Ferrari was stumbling again.

Monza brought the team yet another gift courtesy of McLaren, as Hakkinen selected first gear prematurely going into the first chicane on the 30th lap and spun into tearful retirement. But yet again Irvine was not in a position to capitalise fully. Outqualified again by an on-form Salo, he was only eighth fastest in practice and was unhappy with his car throughout.

'Basically we haven't made enough progress with our car in the past three or four races,' he said philosophically, aware that modifications in the pipeline for the F399 might just come too late. The cynics who subscribed to the theory that Ferrari really did want Schumacher to be its first driving champion since Scheckter went into overdrive.

Salo took his second podium place, finishing a good third behind Frentzen and Ralf Schumacher, which in itself betrayed Ferrari's lack of progress. But Irvine had a troubled run to sixth, his car behaving poorly over Monza's numerous kerbs which are best attacked. He got a point, to draw himself level with Hakkinen at the top of the title table, but he was the first to admit it: 'We got out of jail today.'

Now there were three races left, and the rumours mounted of a behind-the-scenes argument between Ferrari and Michael Schumacher. The team was pushing for its star to return as swiftly as possible, but Monza came and went without him, and so would the last European GP of the 20th century, a race that would have been tailor made for his wet-road artistry.

In the end, a finely judged win went to Johnny Herbert whose Stewart-Ford would start 14th on the grid. But many could have won. Heinz-Harald Frentzen started from pole and led until an electrical malfunction after his pit stop; David Coulthard led then, but crashed; Ralf Schumacher led but picked up a puncture; Giancarlo Fisichella led but crashed.

But what of Ferrari, on a day when Hakkinen was delayed and struggled to beat Marc Gene's Minardi for fifth place? Another day when a win should have gone to Maranello?

Eddie qualified only ninth, Mika, in his last scheduled outing, 12th. Irvine screwed up one run with traffic, and what should have been his best, with a spin; once again he had not delivered when the chips were down. In the race, however, it was Ferrari that engineered the farce. It began when Salo stopped for a new nose on the 20th lap, and took on wet tyres as a light rain continued to make the track slippery. But no sooner had he rejoined, suddenly aware that the switch had been a mistake as the rain eased, than Irvine radioed ahead that he was coming in. A set of wets was ready and waiting, but Eddie said he wanted a fresh set of dries. By the time he arrived, the right rear had gone missing. Mechanics scrambled everywhere in panic, and the red car was stationary for a fraction under 30

As Irvine's F399 hopped inelegantly over the kerbs at Monza, he could feel the world title slipping through Ferrari's fingers.

seconds. It was the worst pit stop of the season. Eddie fell from fifth to 13th, too far behind even to catch the Minardi for sixth place. He was still a second and a half shy when the flag fell, seventh place marking the first time since Imola that he had failed to score points.

It was time for Ferrari's 'secret weapon'. The story goes that when Luca di Montezemolo called Michael Schumacher to inquire after his health (and by inference to find out when he felt like returning to work), Schumacher's daughter Gina Maria informed the Ferrari president that 'Daddy is in the garden, playing football'. This did not go down well with a man watching his team's aspirations slowly melting.

Whatever, Schumacher was back for the inaugural Malaysian GP, looking none the worse for wear. And, suddenly, Ferrari's pace picked up so dramatically upon his return that he took pole position by a clear second from Irvine. The Ulsterman's newfound speed was impressive enough, but nobody could understand where Schumacher found his time; least of all McLaren.

The race story is simply told. Schumacher led for the first three laps before handing over to Irvine. As the Ulsterman sped away to the fourth and final victory of his Ferrari career,

Schumacher spent the rest of his afternoon making Hakkinen's life hell, brake testing the Finn, weaving unpredictably and generally preventing him from having any chance of going after Irvine. Some felt it was brilliant strategy, rather like the tactics Ferrari had told Salo to use at Spa when he persistently delayed a threatening Ralf Schumacher so that Irvine could stop again for fuel without losing fourth place. Others wondered just how much lower Schumacher was prepared to go on the race track.

Schumacher's long-awaited return to F1 duty came in Malaysia. Here he demonstrates to David Coulthard the sort of hard tactics he would later use to torment Mika Hakkinen all afternoon in Sepang, although the Scot made this bold move stick, to snatch second place.

But there was a sting in the tail of this one. As Irvine headed off for a holiday before the title showdown at Suzuka, word came through that both Ferraris had failed a post-race scrutineering check. Their aerodynamic barge boards along the lower sides of the cockpit just aft of the front wheels, did not comply with the regulations. The red cars were out.

At a stroke Irvine's newly minted four-point advantage over Hakkinen was eradicated, together with Ferrari's similar margin over McLaren. An appeal was lodged immediately.

What happened next was the sort of thing that gave rise to allegations that Ferrari enjoyed special status with F1's powers-that-be. In order to have a definitive ruling prior to Suzuka, a fortnight hence, the appeal hearing was set for the following Friday, in Paris (although it would drag on to Saturday). But stories circulated that FIA technical delegate Peter Wright was dispatched to Maranello the Monday after the race with specific instructions to find a reason why the

Ferraris were legal, rather than to investigate whether they actually were. If they weren't, then the championship fight was already over. Irvine would now have 60 points to Hakkinen's 72.

To nobody's surprise, Ferrari achieved what so few before it had ever done, and won its appeal at the Place de la Concorde. FIA president Max Mosley explained patiently that while there were, of course, rules governing dimensions (in a sport in which the designers were increasingly having such things mandated by the legislators), some fell into the category whereby the dimension was a maximum or a minimum, others where the dimension itself was specific and precise. He explained that Ferrari had successfully argued that the barge board dimension fell into the latter,

fixed, category, but that in that case it should therefore be allowed a standard tolerance. McLaren (and Stewart-Ford, which faced losing upgraded second and third places) argued that such a tolerance did not apply, and were not alone in condemning (in private) the whole means by which the case had been heard. Ron Dennis pointed out that in the past any breach of the technical regulations during a race had always been dealt with by the exclusion of the vehicle concerned, well remembering how Hakkinen had lost fourth place at Spa in 1997 for a fuel infringement. But the fact remained, Eddie Irvine and Ferrari headed to Suzuka four points better off than Mika Hakkinen and McLaren. The case was closed.

Psychologically, Hakkinen had the

It's over. On the podium in Suzuka, winner and World Champion Mika Hakkinen acknowledges the fight Eddie Irvine put up all season.

Japanese GP won long before the red starting lights went out, for Irvine crashed heavily in qualifying. Schumacher set the track alight with a scorching pole position ahead of Hakkinen (whose final effort was spoiled when he and Jean Alesi fell over each other) and Coulthard, but Irvine was a subdued fifth, a second and a half off Michael's time, using the spare car after his shunt under braking for the Spoon Curve did heavy damage to his race chassis.

Hakkinen snatched the lead immediately, and only surrendered it during the fuel stops, leaving Schumacher to chase him home and with no need to keep a weather eye in his mirrors for an impatient team-mate. Eddie bounced ahead of Coulthard and Frentzen at the start, moved up to third place when an unusually quick Olivier Panis quit with gearbox failure on his Prost, and then stayed there. The status quo of F1 had effectively been restored, and with no prospect of passing Hakkinen, Irvine was obliged to resign himself to honourable runner-up status after the best season of his career. Yet some wondered why Schumacher, normally so fast around this tricky venue, had been so ineffective in the early stages as Hakkinine headed for the tall timber. Had Michael won, Mika would have taken six points, leaving him with 72. Irvine's four-point haul for third would thus have been sufficient to boost his score to 74, making him champion. Later, Schumacher would complain bitterly that Coulthard had delayed him while being lapped. In truth the incident did nothing whatsoever to change the outcome of the race, and Schumacher's feeble opening pace was never satisfactorily explained.

While Michael was left to ponder what might have been – had he not crashed at Silverstone he would have stood an excellent chance of winning the title, given McLaren's subsequent problems – some wondered if his failure to challenge Hakkinen for victory wasn't the pay-off for what they believed to be the move by which Irvine duped him into his moment of rashness in the fateful British GP. Perhaps there were Machiavellian things at work, perhaps it was all in the imagination and things really were what they seemed to be on the surface. We shall probably never know.

Ferrari had come close enough to win the World Championship for Constructors, its first since 1983, but Mika Hakkinen got to smoke the cigar.

The last word fell to di Montezemolo, who went to Suzuka for the showdown. Hurt by suggestions that Ferrari had not given Irvine 100 per cent support, he said: 'How can anyone really believe that Ferrari would do less than its very best for its drivers? Ferrari always wants to win.'

But rounding out an acrimonious season, he fired a broadside at McLaren and the attitude the British team had taken after the Great Malaysian Controversy.

'I didn't like the way McLaren responded,' he said. 'I didn't like what was said about our cars by people who don't know how to lose.'

Ferrari might, in turn, corporately have been accused of not knowing how to win, but the 2000 season would change all that …

Chapter 7

Double top

Like Enzo Ferrari before him, Luca di Montezemolo, who took over as the president of Scuderia Ferrari in 1992 after the turmoil of the immediate post-Prost era at the end of 1991, rarely makes public appearances at race tracks. And this charismatic man freely admits that he can hardly ever bring himself to watch a race in company.

'When everybody from the factory, God willing, is able to relax at weekends, I am really under pressure when I am alone at my home, watching the race on television,' he says, spreading his hands as if to ask, what can I do?

'I feel very, very emotional, and this is why I cannot watch a race with anybody. I have to watch it alone. That is the moment when I really feel very, very, very nervous, and I don't want to show it to anybody. This is the reason why I am alone.'

Di Montezemolo is the man in the hottest seat at Ferrari, just as he was back in the mid-1970s when he and Niki Lauda helped to drag the team back from the abyss. 'I have known F1 situations since then,' he said with a smile, as Ferrari prepared for yet another new season. 'But now is harder. In 1997 we were competitive against Williams, since then against McLaren. I hope … I'm sure, that we will again be competitive. I don't know at what level, I don't know against whom. But now Ferrari is very competitive.

Unashamedly, the team under di Montezemolo is encouraged to remember its glittering past while looking to its future. 'For me the human resources are critical,' he insists. 'The atmosphere is extremely important. I want people, first of all, who love Ferrari and are totally able to have a team attitude to work. I don't want just kings and heroes, because that is not possible any more. You need people able to work together. And I need people that, of course, have a lot of respect for our past but also look ahead. The past is the lessons for the future. I need to take a lot of care of the past, but I don't want people who look at it and stop. They must also look to the future without being married to the past. The past is the past, important as a point of reference.'

When he returned to the fold, di Montezemolo set about a complete restructure of the Ferrari F1 team. A succession of road car engineers had been placed in charge of running the team in the wake of Enzo Ferrari's death in August 1988. By the end of 1991, when they had sought to assuage public criticism of their feeble style by sacking Alain Prost, one of the few people in Maranello who seemed to know what they were doing, Ferrari was in parlous state. Since Ayrton Senna had removed Prost from contention for the 1990 World Championship by the simple expedient of driving both of them off the road in Suzuka at the end of a bitter season-long conflict, Ferrari had not looked remotely like winning a race. Morale was lower even than it had been the last time that di Montezemolo had been put in charge, late in 1973. He faced a mountain of Everest proportions.

'I told the critics, okay, but I have to prepare for the future. That was the right moment to change, because we were not competitive. It is much better to refresh the house when the weather outside is bad, than to wait for the good weather. So we took the opportunity at the beginning of the 1990s to reorganise, to invest a lot in new technology. Now we have the advantage of what we have done three, four years ago, particularly in advanced technology. But you cannot do this in 12 months. It takes longer to change method, atmo-

Schumacher began 2000 as he meant to carry on, with wins in Australia and Brazil. Here he prepares to share the third, on Ferrari's home ground in Imola, with his delighted team.

sphere, level of the people, speciality of the people. Formula One you can like or not like, but it is a super-specific job. Don't forget that we came from a strong mechanical know-how, so it was important to keep that but to add aerodynamics, electronics, Formula One fighter attitude, and teamwork attitude. Today, I am very proud to have a team which is still very Italian, but also very 'English'. With Italian creativity, mentality and approach, but with some key English people. I am very, very pleased. I am very proud of the whole team. It is like a child for me, I have seen it maturing step-by-step, growing up, the technicians, the mechanics, the new areas: metallurgic, aerodynamic; the engine.'

When di Montezemolo returned to the fold in 1992, the situation was critical. The boom of the 1980s had given way to a car market strangled by world recession. It spread to the team's F1 programme. In 1992, Ferrari scored only 23 points; in 1993, 28. Even before the last race in 1998, it had amassed 127, the highest score in its history.

By the end of the 1999 season, di Montezemolo had been back for seven years, but all there was to show were near misses in the chase for the all-important World Championship for Drivers, and success in the World Championship for Constructors. What Ferrari achieved in the latter in 1999 should not be ignored, but to anyone but a team in F1 it is at best a consola-

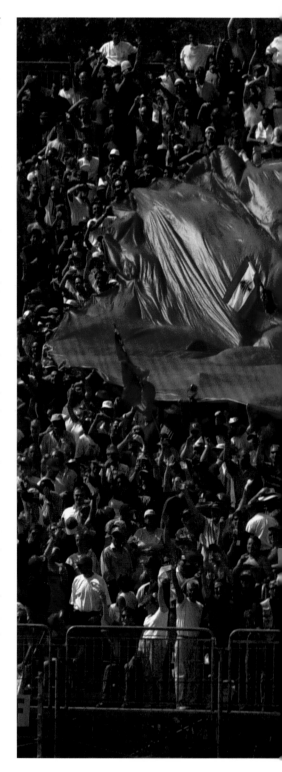

The tifosi recognised a good thing when they saw it, and at Imola the Ferrari flag paid tribute to their unswerving support.

tion prize. The Italian media wanted a lot more. It has never been bird-mouthed with its criticism, and as di Montezemolo and Ferrari faced the first season of the new millennium they had reached a crossroads; failure just wasn't an option.

Under his guidance Ferrari has become a multi-national F1 team

What had gone on behind the scenes at Maranello for the past seven seasons amounted to a quiet revolution, however. The Ferrari of old was riddled with emotion and polemics. If the team won races, its joy knew no bounds. If it lost, wrists were slashed. It was one thing or the other, the emotion always at either end of the spectrum. And when it failed, axes were sharpened. Who was to blame? It smacked of Enzo Ferrari's own Machiavellian approach, where whispers and grassing on others was encouraged. Di Montezemolo changed all that. Under his guidance Ferrari has become a true multi-national F1 team, like all the others, without losing its essential charisma. The first master-stroke had been to bring former Peugeot race team director Jean Todt in as sporting director in 1992. Then had come the Schumacher, Brawn, Byrne triumvirate.

'I saw people coming basically from Fiat,' he said of the early days of his comeback. 'Fantastic company, and at the beginning of the Nineties extremely competitive in rallying with Fiat and Lancia. But that was nothing to do with Formula One. So, to increase the know-how of the company, you have to bring specific people to be in charge of some areas in which you are weak. We are now 420–430 in racing, engine, chassis, gearbox, testing. I think at the end of the day we have got 10–15 foreign people. Okay, you can answer to me, "But they are in key positions". This is correct, particularly in the design of the car. But do you know a car designer who is not English, or not born in the English environment, around Britain's "Silicon Valley"? But now, for instance, we have in aerodynamics, all Italians now that Willem Toet has left. In the last four years we have introduced very young guys, who are now growing up.

'I like the provincial attitude, though I don't mean the closed mind. Opening the mind to new methods and experience is something that we have to do, looking ahead. So we have gone step-by-step. My objective was to put Ferrari at the top level. It is not enough, but I think we have done a lot.

'For me, the Ferrari badge is the most important element. Looking back on 1998 and 1999 we have done a fantastic season. Today, Ferrari is a good team, with no polemics.'

That in itself was quite remarkable, given the passion with which Italians traditionally approach competition. At one time nobody could ever have envisaged a Ferrari where internecine power struggles were not part of the infrastructure. Sir Frank Williams was one of the first outsiders who truly appreciated the threat, back at the end of another successful season for his team in 1996. 'Ferrari is the team I most fear,' he said. 'Look at their level of investment. They are going to take things to a new level.'

They were prescient words, and Sir Frank was proved correct. Together with McLaren, Ferrari had taken things on to a completely new plane.

Gianni Agnelli had put further pressure on di Montezemolo and the team in 1998 when, perhaps unwittingly, perhaps deliberately, he had declared at the unveiling of the new cars that everything had been done to create the best machine for Michael Schumacher, and that Ferrari would have only itself to blame if it did not win the World Championship.

Whether it was just the Fiat patri-arch's unalloyed enthusiasm, or there was a more pointed intention was a moot point. The Italian press picked up on his words, and so did the rest of the world. It was as if the team had been given notice: win, or else. The whole world, it seemed, was growing ever more impatient for Ferrari's first World Championship for Drivers since Jody Scheckter's, all the way back in 1979.

Although Ferrari did fail that year, it could be forgiven for feeling aggrieved at the way things had panned out in 1999. If Schumacher had not crashed at Silverstone, it's hard to see how they could have failed, given the chapter of incidents that befell McLaren and Mercedes-Benz.

In the old days there would have been yet further blood letting, and true to tradition the Italian press was call-

Schumacher's early run was interrupted by a rash of mid-season problems, such as this one in Germany where he heads for the tyre wall at the start after being nerfed by Giancarlo Fisichella.

ing for Todt's head on a block at intervals that were so regular that the little Frenchman ceased to pay the slightest attention. If football managers in the UK think they have a hard time, they should try managing Ferrari.

Inside Maranello, the latest failure merely acted as a spur to greater effort as the team regrouped around the new cleanly titled F1-2000 chassis from Rory Byrne and Ross Brawn. There were no public recriminations, and whatever anyone within the team might have been thinking, outward unity was maintained. This was no easy task, when you consider the scope for argument. Schumacher could have blamed the team for the weeping brake bleed nipple which the latter admitted had been the cause of his crash; likewise he could have blamed Todt for failing to inform him in time that the race had been red flagged. In former times, factors within Ferrari would certainly have accused him of a rash attempt to overtake teammate Eddie Irvine, and then of taking his time before returning to active duty. But there was none of this. The men in red simply banded together more closely, and looked to the future. This, as much as Maranello's technical might and Michael's undisputed driving genius, was what gave McLaren the gravest concern.

The media tried its best to squeeze comments from Todt, but he merely reiterated di Montezemolo's comments. 'You know,' he said firmly, 'the thing that most surprises people outside of Ferrari is that we no longer have any polemics.'

But as the Australian GP at

On the track it was left to Rubens Barrichello to pick up the pieces for Ferrari, and to take advantage of extraordinary circumstances, to score the first GP win of his career.

Melbourne approached in March 2000, the time had come to deliver.

After all the posturing of new car launches and the sabre-rattling of winter testing, it emerged in Melbourne's Albert Park that the McLaren-Mercedes MP4/15 was still the quickest car. Hakkinen took pole position with 1m 30.548s, but Schumacher was only half a second slower, and right behind Coulthard. And when it came to the race it was the Ferrari that held the advantage. Not in terms of raw performance, for the McLarens pulled away initially, but in race speed allied to reliability. Coulthard's engine broke on the 11th lap and Hakkinen's followed suit only seven laps later. Schumacher romped home the easy winner, followed by his new team-mate, Rubens Barrichello.

The dramatic reversal left Ferrari 16 points ahead of McLaren in the constructors' table.

Schumacher won again in Brazil, too, again giving best to the McLarens in qualifying. In the race he grabbed the lead from Hakkinen at the start of the second lap, but both Ferrari drivers were on two-stop refuelling strategies. When the race had stabilised, Hakkinen had a handy lead until his engine once again scattered on the 27th lap. Coulthard finished second on the road but was disqualified for a front wing endplate infringement, and Ferrari's day was only spoiled when Barrichello lost his hydraulic pressure and had to retire after 20 laps.

Yet again Hakkinen took pole position on Ferrari's home ground in Imola, as the circus returned to Europe, but

It was a deeply emotional Brazilian who wept atop the podium, clutching his national flag and flanked by McLaren drivers Hakkinen and Coulthard.

the race belonged to Schumacher once more after some excellent pit strategy employed by Ross Brawn. This time the Finn finished second, but Schumacher and Ferrari were beginning to look very comfortable at the top of the points table.

The clever strategy was combined with some great pitwork that laid the ghost of Irvine's Nürburgring disaster the previous year, and Schumacher's excellent driving. Brawn, Ferrari's director of engineering, paid full tribute to his driver's role in such carefully crafted races. 'Michael's speed is vital,' he said. 'He can make some strategies work that other drivers couldn't make work. Strategy is often an overplayed subject, but with him you can do things and know you have a chance of making them work. We've used some where I'm proud of the races we've done, where we changed the turn of events. He's pretty key to that, an essential ingredient.'

Barrichello had been a rather overshadowed fourth in Imola, but he came into his own at Silverstone, taking pole position as Schumacher had a troubled qualifying session and only lined up fifth on the grid. Worse still for the championship leader, as Barrichello accelerated into the lead, he found newcomer Jenson Button edging confidently alongside going into Copse. With Jacques Villeneuve also making a trademark fast start in the BAR-Honda, Schuey momentarily found

himself down in eighth place. While it was one of Schumacher's least convincing performances, it was one of Barrichello's best as he led until the 35th lap, when another hydraulic glitch caused him to spin before pitting to retire. Schuey's championship luck was evident in the way in which he still finished third despite his early problems, but Coulthard and Hakkinen signalled McLaren's resurgence with a solid 1–2. They went on to repeat that in Spain, with Hakkinen taking his first win of the season, and again it was Barrichello who bought home the bacon for Ferrari with third place. But Schumacher could have won. This was the race in which the German ran ahead of the McLarens initially, after taking pole position. It was a sign that Ferrari could truly hack it with McLaren, albeit a team affected by

Schumacher kept his title aspirations on track with a strong victory in the inaugural US GP at Indianapolis. Here he slithers round the outside of jump-starting Coulthard, going into the first turn.

Hakkinen's lacklustre performances at this point.

Unfortunately, when Michael made his first pit stop he was waved out a fraction too soon, knocking down chief mechanic and head refueller Nigel Stepney. The corollary of this was not immediately apparent, as he continued to lead, but when he came in for his second stop Stepney was in the medical centre having an injured ankle attended to. The stop was catastrophic. Already panicked by Stepney's injury, and now without its regular refueller, the team performed poorly. Hakkinen went into the lead, and then Coulthard, who had already overtaken Barrichello, finally found a way past Michael at the end of the main straight. The Ferrari wasn't as good on its final set of tyres, and Michael was struggling. Eventually a slow puncture was discov-

ered. It was while fighting with brother Ralf, who was not in the mood to be kind, that Michael was overtaken by Barrichello, who slipped by on the inside as the two brothers rubbed wheels in a right-hander. Immediately afterwards Michael pitted for a fresh tyre, and resumed to finish fifth. In view of his adventures, two points could be considered damage limitation.

Now the gap between Schumacher and Hakkinen was 16 points, but Michael hit back with a fine win on a slippery track at the Nürburgring, where Rubens was fourth behind the McLarens.

So now the stage was set for Monte Carlo, where Schumacher and Ferrari celebrated his 18-point series lead by taking pole position. But this time the regular pattern of 2000 was broken by the presence of Jarno Trulli on the

front row in his Jordan Mugen Honda, and Frentzen alongside Coulthard on row two. Hakkinen was still in his fallow period, taking fifth place ahead of Barrichello. Far from being reeled in as the McLarens hit their stride, Ferrari still had the upper hand. And far from Hakkinen providing the main challenge, it was Coulthard who posed the greater threat. Michael could have been forgiven for feeling complacent as he stormed into the lead and left Coulthard to try to find a way by Trulli as Frentzen kept Hakkinen bottled up.

Only team orders kept Ferrari number four in second place

What happened next remains open to conjecture. According to Ferrari, a broken exhaust overheated carbon fibre composites in the car's rear suspension; according to Mika Salo, Michael walloped a wall. The upshot was that he was forced to retire with damaged suspension on the 55th lap, losing an easy 10 points. Barrichello was second, however, and with Hakkinen finishing a troubled sixth as Coulthard won, things were not as bad as they could have been.

In Canada, Schumacher made up for his gaffe in the previous year's race with another victory, but on this occasion Barrichello had the legs of him in the rain and closed a large gap to nothing. Only team orders kept Ferrari number four in second place in line astern of

number three as they crossed the finish line, a tenth of a second apart.

Coulthard was again the stronger McLaren, but killed his chances after stalling on the grid for the formation lap and being penalised subsequently after his mechanics had worked to fire his car up more than 15 seconds after the allotted time allowance. Hakkinen couldn't manage better than fourth, so now the McLaren drivers had 34 and 32 points respectively, to Schumacher's 56. But just as things seemed rosy again for Ferrari, they were about to start going badly wrong.

In France, Schumacher and Barrichello reminded everyone of Ferrari's growing strength with first and third fastest practice times, but then Michael was beaten in a straight fight by Coulthard in the race, from which he retired on the 59th lap with a rare failure of Paolo Martinelli's excellent but unsung V10 engine. As Coulthard swept home ahead of Hakkinen, to remain the greater threat to Schumacher, Barrichello took the final podium place.

As he left France, Schumacher could not know that this was just the start of his problems. In both Austria and Germany he suffered a first-corner retirement.

In qualifying at Spielberg he struggled to get his F1-2000 set up properly and lined up only fourth, alongside Barrichello and behind the McLaren front row. To make matters worse, Hakkinen was at last back on the form everyone had come to expect, taking pole position comfortably from Coulthard. In a dismal weekend, Michael's only consolation would be that he had said all along that Mika was the real challenge he feared, not David. And as Mika returned to form, so David seemed to become out-psyched again.

At the start, sixth fastest Ricardo Zonta hit the back of Michael's car heading for the uphill first corner, spinning it into Rubens's path. When Jarno Trulli, fifth on the grid, arrived, he too had to go off the track to avoid the carnage, and hit the front of the Ferrari. Both were instant retirements, but Barrichello carried on to finish third after a strong recovery.

Schumacher was highly critical of Zonta afterwards, but some observers took the view that the incident had its roots in Schumacher's own poor start and Barrichello's apparent wish to defer to his team-mate at the first corner. The field bunched as he waited for the tardy German to hit his stride. 'Certainly,' Zonta said in his own defence, 'Michael didn't seem to get off the line as fast as I had expected him too.'

Suddenly, Schumacher had only a six-point lead over Coulthard, and Hakkinen was fast moving up and only two points further adrift. For Ferrari the only bright spot came when Hakkinen's car was inspected after the race and it was discovered that one of the seals had fallen off the FIA's onboard 'black box'. McLaren subsequently was denied its 10 points for a victory that had signalled that the

Moment of truth: in past seasons Schumacher had shown signs of strain at the start of the Japanese GP, but this time there would be no pre-match nerves. 'I never drove better in my life', he said after scoring the crucial victory.

2000 World Championship was far from over.

So to Hockenheim, where Michael was beaten to pole position by Coulthard as Giancarlo Fisichella sneaked ahead of Hakkinen for third on the grid. Afloat on a sea of troubles, Barrichello had an appalling time in qualifying and was only 18th in the lineup.

In a flash, the Ferrari was spun out of the race by the Benetton

There was a backdrop to what happened at the start, which had it roots in Schumacher's starts in 1999 and, specifically, since Imola, in 2000. There, and many times subsequently, the German had taken to weaving violently on leaving the startline, to frustrate overtaking attempts by his rivals. To a man they were all getting pretty fed up with the tactic, and among them, both Coulthard and Jacques Villeneuve had called on the FIA to make a proper ruling on what was permissible. Once again the governing body fumbled the chance to instil a degree of discipline into what was becoming an increasingly unruly part of each race (the fear of a shunt was so great at Spa, for example, that the damp race would start behind the safety car). Instead, in a half-hearted ruling, it condoned the behaviour, so long as the swoop was unidirectional. In practice, what this meant was that

Schumacher would sweep a rival wide by moving in one direction, then take his optimum line into the corner, which comprised another change of direction.

Coulthard had certainly had enough of all this nit-picking, and in Germany gave back to Schumacher what Michael had himself dished out so often. Swooping across the Ferrari's bows, DC obliged Michael to back off just as Fisichella was getting into his stride. In a flash, the Ferrari was spun out of the race by the Benetton as Hakkinen gratefully swept inside them all to snatch the lead.

For 24 laps Schumacher had the mental anguish of knowing Mika was right up at the front, all the time eroding his points lead. But out on the track he had an unexpected ally. Robert Sehli was a disgruntled former employee of Mercedes-Benz in France. Having attempted fruitlessly to voice his complaint over dismissal at the French GP, and been turfed off the grid at Hockenheim, he now wandered out into the woods. Just as it began to rain, this polythene raincoat-clad figure could be seen walking alongside the track as he waved at the cars; it was an extraordinary scene. Nobody could be sure that he was not intent on a particularly gruesome and selfish form of suicide, so out came the safety car to slow the field while he was rounded up.

Now the rain fell more, and Hakkinen sped into the pits for wet

Ferrari's champagne-soaked sporting director, Jean Todt, sees the end of a long road as he hoists his driver aloft during their triumphant celebrations.

tyres. Coulthard could not do so because McLaren could not service both cars at once, and the delay of doing a wet lap on dry tyres, and then stopping for wets next time around, would kill his chances. He would have to be content with third place. Ferrari now enacted some masterful strategy to take advantage of this sudden turn of events. As the race progressed only half of the track was wet, so dry tyres were not a complete disadvantage. Indeed, Hakkinen's lap times and Barrichello's were pretty much even. So Ross Brawn and Rubens Barrichello decided not to stop. Rubens would have to work hard to avoid mistakes on the wet section, but equally, Hakkinen was having to avoid overheating his wets on the dry part.

The gamble paid off handsomely, as the tearful Brazilian stood atop the podium celebrating the first victory of his F1 career, and a fine bit of damage limitation.

Schumacher was now on his back foot, with both Coulthard and Hakkinen only two points behind, but hit his stride again with pole position in Hungary. The Finn confirmed his return however, with a stunningly opportunistic overtaking move going into the first corner which won him the race on a track where passing is all but impossible. Michael fended off David's threats all through the race, but left Hungary without the lead in the title points chase. Now Mika had 64 to his 62 and David's 58. Ferrari was on the run.

Schumacher's expression on the podium in Belgian said it all as he could

Back in Maranello, the tifosi were not slow to stage their own celebrations, which included the questionable taste of giving McLaren's title hopes a decent burial.

The photo that says it all: 21 years after Jody Scheckter won the crown at Monza, Ferrari can finally celebrate once again life at the summit of the F1 mountain.

see his chances of a first Ferrari title slipping away. In the race of the season he had qualified only fourth, separated from Hakkinen by emergent upstarts Jarno Trulli and Jenson Button, and that was where he stayed as the race began behind the safety car. But when Button and Trulli tangled as the racing really got under way, he slipped up to chase the McLaren. His persistence paid off when Hakkinen put a wheel over the slippery kerb at Blanchimont on the 11th lap, and almost spun in the circuit's fastest corner. But Mika made the save of the season and started to come back at Michael. Initially the latter seemed set for another win, but bit by bit Mika came back at him. Within four laps of the finish Hakkinen

slipped alongside on the fast run up to Les Combes at the top of the circuit, only to be rebuffed so resolutely by Schumacher at more than 180mph (290kph) that the McLaren's left front wing endplate bore signs of tyre scuffs from the Ferrari's right rear wheel.

A lap later they came upon Zonta's BAR as they sped back up to Les Combes. Just before the corner, Schumacher jinked left to pass the white car. Summoning everything he had, Hakkinen slammed down the inside of it, on the right, only milli-metres from the grass, and as the two rivals emerged ahead of the startled Brazilian, Hakkinen had the lead.

Suddenly, the World Championship race had distilled to a two-horse affair between Hakkinen and Schumacher, with Coulthard able to muster no better than fourth place, and it looked as if the tide was finally running with McLaren. Five disastrous races had hobbled Ferrari, and thoughts of failure flitted through Maranello like spectres.

The pressure on the Scuderia can be imagined. It had led the chase all season, had a car that was demonstrably as quick as the McLaren in qualifying, and whose only problem was that it was less kind to its tyres in races than the MP4/15 was. That meant that Michael and Rubens often had to qualify on Bridgestone's harder rubber since teams must race on what they select for qualifying, yet still the F1-2000 was capable of taking pole positions. And now came the biggest race of Ferrari's year, on home ground at Monza. A failure there would have a devastating effect on morale, regardless of how polemically free the team was.

At the press conference he broke down and wept uncontrollably

The red men struck a vital psychological blow when Schumacher and Barrichello wrapped up the front row in qualifying, leaving Hakkinen third and separated from shotgun Coulthard by upstart Jacques Villeneuve in the improving BAR-Honda. The race would be overshadowed by the accident involving Coulthard, Barrichello and the two Jordans in the second chicane during the opening lap, but Schumacher and Ferrari blended excellent tactics with some more fine driving to beat Hakkinen and McLaren, and thrust themselves right back into title contention.

As he considered how his performance had won him his 41st Grand Prix, bringing him level with Ayrton Senna's score, and moved him back to within two points of Mika Hakkinen, it all became too much for Schumacher. At the post-race press conference he broke down and wept uncontrollably, consoled in varying measures by Hakkinen and bother Ralf, who had finished a fine third.

'I think it is obvious why I am so emotional,' Schumacher managed to say. 'The victory was here in Italy in front of the Ferrari home crowd, and we have obviously been in some difficulty over the past few races where we haven't been on the pace.'

But now Ferrari was back on target. 'This success simply came a lot more close to me – I cannot put it into words,' Schumacher finished.

It was amid much fanfare that F1 made its return to North America after an absence of nine years, and the locals were much cheered to see Schumacher and Ferrari sitting on pole position, even if the grid had to be moved so that Indianapolis's famous line of bricks across the oval track's startline did not impede his chances of a perfect getaway. Coulthard jumped the start and remained in front until Schumacher finally found a way by going round the outside into the first corner, and as the Scot faded with the inevitable penalty stop, it was

All that remained was to cement victory in the Constructors' Championship, and the red wigs came out again in Sepang as Schumacher and Barrichello (here with Ross Brawn and David Coulthard) achieved a suitable 1–2 result.

Hakkinen who came thrusting up to challenge. The track had been damp at the start, and as it began to dry Hakkinen lost a lot of time behind the Minardis before finally getting into a rhythm that saw him slashing into Schumacher's advantage. The Finn got within five seconds when his Mercedes-Benz engine broke, and even a late spin when he lost concentration could not dislodge a delighted Schumacher.

With two races left, he was back in the lead of the World Championship, eight comfortable points clear. Hakkinen had to win the last two races, with Coulthard (or anyone but Schumacher) second at least once, if he was to score a third consecutive World Championship. It was possible that

Hakkinen could still do it, but although it might not have seemed so the odds favoured Schumacher, who already had seven wins to the Finn's four and was looking strong again. He had only to finish second twice, and if he won the Japanese GP, then it was all over.

For 36 of the 53 laps it appeared that the chase would go down to the wire in Malaysia. Schumacher had taken pole yet again, and administered his now customary swerve and chop to Hakkinen going off the line, but Mika had simply ignored all that in the midst of a blistering start that thrust the McLaren firmly into the lead. The two then dropped Coulthard and Barrichello as their *mano a mano* confrontation developed. Hakkinen led until his first fuel stop on the 21st lap, then resumed the lead when Schumacher stopped for fuel and tyres two laps later and Coulthard had one brief lap in the lead.

It was the perfect ending to a dream season

But as they approached their second stops, it began to rain slightly. On the 36th lap Hakkinen swept in from the lead. He had been coming up on a gaggle of traffic, and it was the perfect time to come into the pits. But then two things happened. Schumacher got the hammer down, as is his habit in such circumstances, and was quicker in the difficult conditions than Hakkinen, whose new tyres were yet to come up to full working temperature. He found himself trapped behind Pedro de la Rosa's soon-to-be-lapped Arrows at the very point when he needed to be flat to the floor to be sure of getting ahead of Schumacher during the Ferrari's stop four laps later.

Michael did not feel he had done enough, especially as he was delayed slightly as Wurz spun his Benetton out of the chicane just as Michael was pitting. 'Ross kept telling me, "It's looking good, looking good,"' Schumacher reported. 'Then he said, "Looking very good." But it wasn't until I was back on the track and Mika hadn't come back past me that I allowed myself to believe that it was true.'

Although Hakkinen fought back and closed the gap to within two seconds by the flag, it was over. And with that Japanese GP so died Ferrari's long wait for absolution – 21 years after Jody Scheckter had clinched the World Championship for Drivers for Ferrari at Monza in 1979, Michael Schumacher had finally secured his third World Championship.

He held his helmeted head in his hands in *parc fermé* as Hakkinen was the first to congratulate him, and emotional scenes followed. Ferrari broke out red wigs to acknowledge the famous testa rossas of yore, and one by one Schumacher embraced members of the team as he walked down the temporary fence separating the pit lane from *parc fermé*. It made fantastic television, especially when he came, almost in surprise, to the one little figure who was not wearing a red wig. Michael embraced his wife Corinna and kissed her, savouring the moment of triumph.

All Ferrari needed now was another four points from the Malaysian GP to retain its World Championship for Constructors. But Schumacher went a lot better than that, winning the race as Hakkinen was penalised for a jump start, and thus equalling his own, and Nigel Mansell's, record of nine wins in a season. It was the perfect ending to a dream season.

The dissection of the championship began almost immediately. What would have happened had Hakkinen been on top form all season? If Mercedes-Benz had not had three crucial engine failures on the Finn's car? What if Ferrari had not succeeded in having McLaren's legal and expen-

Michael Schumacher made no secret of his delight at seeing the number one on his new challenger for 2001, nor his belief that Ferrari was perfectly poised to continue its domination.

sively developed torque-steer differentials outlawed after all (the way it had brake steer banned in 1998)? What if Bridgestone had not taken the unusual decision to supply only one tyre compound in Japan, a factor that undoubtedly played into Ferrari's hands?

Cut it how you liked, the 2000 World Championship was no dull affair, and there were no simple answers to the myriad questions. Hakkinen and McLaren could have won, perhaps they even should have won, but this was also Ferrari's most convincing performance in a long time. The team had been tested severely, but it made the grade. Schumacher took nine pole positions and nine victories, was second twice, third and fifth once apiece, and set three fastest laps on his way to 108 points. Barrichello backed him well, taking that inaugural win and backing it with one pole, four second places, four thirds and four fourths, and another three fastest laps. With 62 points he finished fourth in the title chase, but made a significant contribution to the 170 points that ensured Ferrari its constructors' victory over McLaren.

But there was no doubt that once all of Luca di Montezemolo's tactical reorganisation had been taken into account, together with Jean Todt's brilliant management, Ross Brawn and Rory Byrne's engineering skills and Paol Martinelli's fabulous little engine, Michael Schumacher was the key. When he couldn't win he never gave up, he never gave less than his best (even at Silverstone where he salvaged a podium place without seeming to do anything special), and he retained his focus and composure even during the tough times.

'Even weeks after winning the title for Ferrari, I still have trouble finding the right words,' he admitted. 'We tried for so long, and we came so close so many times. But those disappointments only make this success better. Nobody can deny that Ferrari is different to other teams. It is special. And this success is a just reward for all the work that has been invested for so long by people who love this sport.'

And the future? There was been much speculation that the Schumacher, Brawn, Byrne triumvirate might break up, Michael and Rory pondering retirement, Ross a new challenge at Jaguar. Todt and di Montezemolo have also hinted that life might now offer different things. But they all seem likely to stay together for at least another season, defending their championship crowns.

Perhaps Brawn summed it all up best.

'I came here to win the World Championship for Ferrari, so in one sense it is mission accomplished,' he said. 'I have achieved championships before, with Benetton, but Ferrari is an ultimate and the passion and determination is just as strong do it again in 2001.

'I don't know whether this success will make the pressure greater or less. We'll have to see what develops. I think it could be more, because everyone will expect us to do it again. But a lot of the pressure you create comes from yourself.'

Appendix 1

Ferrari –
race results

This accompanying results section gives all the Formula 1 race results achieved by Ferrari Grand Prix cars from the start of the 1988 season through to the final round of the 2000 season.

Key to abbreviations:

D – disqualified; FL – fastest lap;
P – pole position; R – retired

1988

3 Apr	BRAZILIAN GP, Rio de Janeiro		
	M. Alboreto	Ferrari F187/88C	5
	G. Berger	Ferrari F187/88C	2/FL
1 May	SAN MARINO GP, Imola		
	M. Alboreto	Ferrari F187/88C	18/R
	G. Berger	Ferrari F187/88C	5
15 May	MONACO GP, Monte Carlo		
	M. Alboreto	Ferrari F187/88C	3
	G. Berger	Ferrari F187/88C	2
29 May	MEXICO GP, Mexico City		
	M. Alboreto	Ferrari F187/88C	4
	G. Berger	Ferrari F187/88C	3
12 Jun	CANADIAN GP, Montreal		
	M. Alboreto	Ferrari F187/88C	R
	G. Berger	Ferrari F187/88C	R
19 Jun	USA GP, Detroit		
	M. Alboreto	Ferrari F187/88C	R
	G. Berger	Ferrari F187/88C	R
3 Jul	FRENCH GP, Paul Ricard		
	M. Alboreto	Ferrari F187/88C	3
	G. Berger	Ferrari F187/88C	4
10 Jul	BRITISH GP, Silverstone		
	M. Alboreto	Ferrari F187/88C	17/R
	G. Berger	Ferrari F187/88C	P/9
24 Jul	GERMAN GP, Hockenheim		
	M. Alboreto	Ferrari F187/88C	4
	G. Berger	Ferrari F187/88C	3
7 Aug	HUNGARIAN GP, Hungaroring		
	M. Alboreto	Ferrari F187/88C	R
	G. Berger	Ferrari F187/88C	4
28 Aug	BELGIAN GP, Spa-Francorchamps		
	M. Alboreto	Ferrari F187/88C	R
	G. Berger	Ferrari F187/88C	R/FL
11 Sep	ITALIAN GP, Monza		
	M. Alboreto	Ferrari F187/88C	2/FL
	G. Berger	Ferrari F187/88C	1
25 Sep	PORTUGUESE GP, Estoril		
	M. Alboreto	Ferrari F187/88C	5
	G. Berger	Ferrari F187/88C	R/FL

2 Oct SPANISH GP, Jerez de la Frontera
M. Alboreto Ferrari F187/88C R
G. Berger Ferrari F187/88C 6
30 Oct JAPANESE GP, Suzuka
M. Alboreto Ferrari F187/88C 11
G. Berger Ferrari F187/88C 4
13 Nov AUSTRALIAN GP, Adelaide
M. Alboreto Ferrari F187/88C R
G. Berger Ferrari F187/88C R

1989

26 Mar BRAZILIAN GP, Rio de Janeiro
N. Mansell Ferrari 640 1
G. Berger Ferrari 640 R
23 Apr SAN MARINO GP, Imola
N. Mansell Ferrari 640 R
G. Berger Ferrari 640 R
7 May MONACO GP, Monte Carlo
N. Mansell Ferrari 640 R
28 May MEXICAN GP, Mexico City
N. Mansell Ferrari 640 R/FL
G. Berger Ferrari 640 R
4 Jun USA GP, Phoenix
N. Mansell Ferrari 640 R
G. Berger Ferrari 640 R
18 Jun CANADIAN GP, Montreal
N. Mansell Ferrari 640 D
G. Berger Ferrari 640 R
9 Jul FRENCH GP, Paul Ricard
N. Mansell Ferrari 640 2
G. Berger Ferrari 640 R
16 Jul BRITISH GP, Silverstone
N. Mansell Ferrari 640 2/FL
G. Berger Ferrari 640 R
30 Jul GERMAN GP, Hockenheim
N. Mansell Ferrari 640 3
G. Berger Ferrari 640 R
13 Aug HUNGARIAN GP, Hungaroring
N. Mansell Ferrari 640 1/FL
G. Berger Ferrari 640 R
27 Aug BELGIAN GP, Spa-Francorchamps
N. Mansell Ferrari 640 3
G. Berger Ferrari 640 R
10 Sep ITALIAN GP, Monza
N. Mansell Ferrari 640 R
G. Berger Ferrari 640 2

24 Sep PORTUGUESE GP, Estoril
N. Mansell Ferrari 640 R/D
G. Berger Ferrari 640 1/FL
1 Oct SPANISH GP, Jerez de la Frontera
G. Berger Ferrari 640 2
22 Oct JAPANESE GP, Suzuka
N. Mansell Ferrari 640 R
G. Berger Ferrari 640 R
5 Nov AUSTRALIAN GP, Adelaide
N. Mansell Ferrari 640 R
G. Berger Ferrari 640 R

1990

11 Mar USA GP, Phoenix
A. Prost Ferrari 641 R
N. Mansell Ferrari 641 R
25 Mar BRAZILIAN GP, Interlagos
A. Prost Ferrari 641 1
N. Mansell Ferrari 641 4
13 May SAN MARINO GP, Imola
A. Prost Ferrari 641 4
N. Mansell Ferrari 641 R
27 May MONACO GP, Monte Carlo
A. Prost Ferrari 641 R
N. Mansell Ferrari 641 R
10 Jun CANADIAN GP, Montreal
A. Prost Ferrari 641 5
N. Mansell Ferrari 641 3
24 Jun MEXICAN GP, Mexico City
A. Prost Ferrari 641 1/FL
N. Mansell Ferrari 641 2
8 Jul FRENCH GP, Paul Ricard
A. Prost Ferrari 641 1
N. Mansell Ferrari 641 P/18/R/FL
15 Jul BRITISH GP, Silverstone
A. Prost Ferrari 641 1
N. Mansell Ferrari 641 P/R/FL
29 Jul GERMAN GP, Hockenheim
A. Prost Ferrari 641 4
N. Mansell Ferrari 641 R
12 Aug HUNGARIAN GP, Hungaroring
A. Prost Ferrari 641 R
N. Mansell Ferrari 641 17/R
26 Aug BELGIAN GP, Spa-Francorchamps
A. Prost Ferrari 641 2/FL
N. Mansell Ferrari 641 R

9 Sep ITALIAN GP, Monza

A. Prost	Ferrari 641	2
N. Mansell	Ferrari 641	4

23 Sep PORTUGUESE GP, Estoril

A. Prost	Ferrari 641	3
N. Mansell	Ferrari 641	P/1

30 Sep SPANISH GP, Jerez de la Frontera

A. Prost	Ferrari 641	1
N. Mansell	Ferrari 641	2

21 Oct JAPANESE GP, Suzuka

A. Prost	Ferrari 641	R
N. Mansell	Ferrari 641	R

4 Nov AUSTRALIAN GP, Adelaide

A. Prost	Ferrari 641	3
N. Mansell	Ferrari 641	2/FL

1991

10 Mar USA GP, Phoenix

A. Prost	Ferrari 642	2
J. Alesi	Ferrari 642	12/R/FL

24 Mar BRAZILIAN GP, Interlagos

A. Prost	Ferrari 642	4
J. Alesi	Ferrari 642	6

28 Apr SAN MARINO GP, Imola

A. Prost	Ferrari 642	R
J. Alesi	Ferrari 642	R

12 May MONACO GP, Monte Carlo

A. Prost	Ferrari 642	5/FL
J. Alesi	Ferrari 642	3

2 Jun CANADIAN GP, Montreal

A. Prost	Ferrari 642	R
J. Alesi	Ferrari 642	R

16 Jun MEXICAN GP, Mexico City

A. Prost	Ferrari 642	R
J. Alesi	Ferrari 642	R

7 Jul FRENCH GP, Magny-Cours

A. Prost	Ferrari 643	2
J. Alesi	Ferrari 643	4

14 Jul BRITISH GP, Silverstone

A. Prost	Ferrari 643	3
J. Alesi	Ferrari 643	R

28 Jul GERMAN GP, Hockenheim

A. Prost	Ferrari 643	R
J. Alesi	Ferrari 643	3

11 Aug HUNGARIAN GP, Hungaroring

A. Prost	Ferrari 643	R
J. Alesi	Ferrari 643	5

25 Aug BELGIAN GP, Spa-Francorchamps

A. Prost	Ferrari 643	R
J. Alesi	Ferrari 643	R

8 Sep ITALIAN GP, Monza

A. Prost	Ferrari 643	3
J. Alesi	Ferrari 643	R

22 Sep PORTUGUESE GP, Estoril

A. Prost	Ferrari 643	R
J. Alesi	Ferrari 643	3

29 Sep SPANISH GP, Montmelo

A. Prost	Ferrari 643	2
J. Alesi	Ferrari 643	4

20 Oct JAPANESE GP, Suzuka

A. Prost	Ferrari 643	4
J. Alesi	Ferrari 643	R

3 Nov AUSTRALIAN GP, Adelaide

G. Morbidelli	Ferrari 643	6
J. Alesi	Ferrari 643	R

1992

1 Mar SOUTH AFRICAN GP, Kyalami

J. Alesi	Ferrari F92A	R
I. Capelli	Ferrari F92A	R

22 Mar MEXICAN GP, Mexico City

J. Alesi	Ferrari F92A	R
I. Capelli	Ferrari F92A	R

5 Apr BRAZILIAN GP, Interlagos

J. Alesi	Ferrari F92A	4
I. Capelli	Ferrari F92A	5

3 May SPANISH GP, Montmelo

J. Alesi	Ferrari F92A	3
I. Capelli	Ferrari F92A	10/R

17 May SAN MARINO GP, Imola

J. Alesi	Ferrari F92A	R
I. Capelli	Ferrari F92A	R

31 May MONACO GP, Monte Carlo

J. Alesi	Ferrari F92A	R
I. Capelli	Ferrari F92A	R

14 Jun CANADIAN GP, Montreal

J. Alesi	Ferrari F92A	3
I. Capelli	Ferrari F92A	R

5 Jul FRENCH GP, Magny-Cours

J. Alesi	Ferrari F92A	R
I. Capelli	Ferrari F92A	R

12 Jul BRITISH GP, Silverstone

J. Alesi	Ferrari F92A	R
I. Capelli	Ferrari F92A	9

26 Jul	GERMAN GP, Hockenheim		
J. Alesi	Ferrari F92A	5
I. Capelli	Ferrari F92A	R
16 Aug	HUNGARIAN GP, Hungaroring		
J. Alesi	Ferrari F92A	R
I. Capelli	Ferrari F92A	6
30 Aug	BELGIAN GP, Spa-Francorchamps		
J. Alesi	Ferrari F92AT	R
I. Capelli	Ferrari F92A	R
Sep	ITALIAN GP, Monza		
J. Alesi	Ferrari F92AT	R
I. Capelli	Ferrari F92AT	R
27 Sep	PORTUGUESE GP, Estoril		
J. Alesi	Ferrari F92AT	R
I. Capelli	Ferrari F92AT	R
25 Oct	JAPANESE GP, Suzuka		
J. Alesi	Ferrari F92AT	5
N. Larini	Ferrari F9200	12
8 Nov	AUSTRALIAN GP, Adelaide		
J. Alesi	Ferrari F92AT	4
N. Larini	Ferrari F92AT	11

1993

14 Mar	SOUTH AFRICAN GP, Kyalami		
J. Alesi	Ferrari F93A	R
G. Berger	Ferrari F93A	6/R
28 Mar	BRAZILIAN GP, Interlagos		
J. Alesi	Ferrari F93A	8
G. Berger	Ferrari F93A	R
11 Apr	EUROPEAN GP, Donington Park		
J. Alesi	Ferrari F93A	R
G. Berger	Ferrari F93A	R
25 Apr	SAN MARINO GP, Imola		
J. Alesi	Ferrari F93A	R
G. Berger	Ferrari F93A	R
9 May	SPANISH GP, Montmelo		
J. Alesi	Ferrari F93A	R
G. Berger	Ferrari F93A	6
23 May	MONACO GP, Monte Carlo		
J. Alesi	Ferrari F93A	3
G. Berger	Ferrari F93A	14/R
13 Jun	CANADIAN GP, Montreal		
J. Alesi	Ferrari F93A	R
G. Berger	Ferrari F93A	4
4 Jul	FRENCH GP, Magny-Cours		
J. Alesi	Ferrari F93A	R
G. Berger	Ferrari F93A	14

11 Jul	BRITISH GP, Silverstone		
J. Alesi	Ferrari F93A	9
G. Berger	Ferrari F93A	R
25 Jul	GERMAN GP, Hockenheim		
J. Alesi	Ferrari F93A	7
G. Berger	Ferrari F93A	6
15 Aug	HUNGARIAN GP, Hungaroring		
J. Alesi	Ferrari F93A	R
G. Berger	Ferrari F93A	3
29 Aug	BELGIAN GP, Spa-Francorchamps		
J. Alesi	Ferrari F93A	R
G. Berger	Ferrari F93A	10/R
12 Sep	ITALIAN GP, Monza		
J. Alesi	Ferrari F93A	2
G. Berger	Ferrari F93A	R
26 Sep	PORTUGUESE GP, Estoril		
J. Alesi	Ferrari F93A	4
G. Berger	Ferrari F93A	R
24 Oct	JAPANESE GP, Suzuka		
J. Alesi	Ferrari F93A	R
G. Berger	Ferrari F93A	R
7 Nov	AUSTRALIAN GP, Adelaide		
J. Alesi	Ferrari F93A	4
G. Berger	Ferrari F93A	5

1994

27 Mar	BRAZILIAN GP, Interlagos		
J. Alesi	Ferrari 412T1	3
G. Berger	Ferrari 412T1	R
17 Apr	PACIFIC GP, Aida		
N. Larini	Ferrari 412T1	R
G. Berger	Ferrari 412T1	2
1 May	SAN MARINO GP, Imola		
N. Larini	Ferrari 412T1	2
G. Berger	Ferrari 412T1	R
15 May	MONACO GP, Monte Carlo		
J. Alesi	Ferrari 412T1	5
G. Berger	Ferrari 412T1	3
29 May	SPANISH GP, Montmelo		
J. Alesi	Ferrari 412T1	4
G. Berger	Ferrari 412T1	R
12 Jun	CANADIAN GP, Montreal		
J. Alesi	Ferrari 412T1	3
G. Berger	Ferrari 412T1	4
3 Jul	FRENCH GP, Magny-Cours		
J. Alesi	Ferrari 412T1B	R
G. Berger	Ferrari 412T1B	3

10 Jul   BRITISH GP, Silverstone
  J. Alesi   Ferrari 412T1B   2
  G. Berger   Ferrari 412T1B   R
31 Jul   GERMAN GP, Hockenheim
  J. Alesi   Ferrari 412T1B   R
  G. Berger   Ferrari 412T1B   P/1
14 Aug   HUNGARIAN GP, Hungaroring
  J. Alesi   Ferrari 412T1B   R
  G. Berger   Ferrari 412T1B   12/R
28 Aug   BELGIAN GP, Spa-Francorchamps
  J. Alesi   Ferrari 412T1B   R
  G. Berger   Ferrari 412T1B   R
11 Sep   ITALIAN GP, Monza
  J. Alesi   Ferrari 412T1B   P/R
  G. Berger   Ferrari 412T1B   2
25 Sep   PORTUGUESE GP, Estoril
  J. Alesi   Ferrari 412T1B   R
  G. Berger   Ferrari 412T1B   P/R
16 Oct   EUROPEAN GP, Jerez de la Frontera
  J. Alesi   Ferrari 412T1B   10
  G. Berger   Ferrari 412T1B   5
6 Nov   JAPANESE GP, Suzuka
  J. Alesi   Ferrari 412T1B   3
  G. Berger   Ferrari 412T1B   R
13 Nov   AUSTRALIAN GP, Adelaide
  J. Alesi   Ferrari 412T1B   6
  G. Berger   Ferrari 412T1B   2

1995

26 Mar   BRAZILIAN GP, Interlagos
  J. Alesi   Ferrari 412T2   5
  G. Berger   Ferrari 412T2   3
9 Apr   ARGENTINIAN GP, Buenos Aires
  J. Alesi   Ferrari 412T2   2
  G. Berger   Ferrari 412T2   6
30 Apr   SAN MARINO GP, Imola
  J. Alesi   Ferrari 412T2   2
  G. Berger   Ferrari 412T2   3/FL
14 May   SPANISH GP, Montmelo
  J. Alesi   Ferrari 412T2   R
  G. Berger   Ferrari 412T2   3
28 May   MONACO GP, Monte Carlo
  J. Alesi   Ferrari 412T2   R/FL
  G. Berger   Ferrari 412T2   3
11 Jun   CANADIAN GP, Montreal
  J. Alesi   Ferrari 412T2   1
  G. Berger   Ferrari 412T2   11/R

2 Jul   FRENCH GP, Magny-Cours
  J. Alesi   Ferrari 412T2   5
  G. Berger   Ferrari 412T2   12
16 Jul   BRITISH GP, Silverstone
  J. Alesi   Ferrari 412T2   2
  G. Berger   Ferrari 412T2   R
30 Jul   GERMAN GP, Hockenheim
  J. Alesi   Ferrari 412T2   R
  G. Berger   Ferrari 412T2   3
13 Aug   HUNGARIAN GP, Hungaroring
  J. Alesi   Ferrari 412T2   R
  G. Berger   Ferrari 412T2   3
27 Aug   BELGIAN GP, Spa-Francorchamps
  J. Alesi   Ferrari 412T2   R
  G. Berger   Ferrari 412T2   P/R
10 Sep   ITALIAN GP, Monza
  J. Alesi   Ferrari 412T2   R
  G. Berger   Ferrari 412T2   R/FL
24 Sep   PORTUGUESE GP, Estoril
  J. Alesi   Ferrari 412T2   5
  G. Berger   Ferrari 412T2   4
1 Oct   EUROPEAN GP, Nürburgring
  J. Alesi   Ferrari 412T2   2
  G. Berger   Ferrari 412T2   R
22 Oct   PACIFIC GP, Aida
  J. Alesi   Ferrari 412T2   5
  G. Berger   Ferrari 412T2   4
29 Oct   JAPANESE GP, Suzuka
  J. Alesi   Ferrari 412T2   R
  G. Berger   Ferrari 412T2   R
12 Nov   AUSTRALIAN GP, Adelaide
  J. Alesi   Ferrari 412T2   R
  G. Berger   Ferrari 412T2   R

1996

10 Mar   AUSTRALIAN GP, Melbourne
  M. Schumacher   Ferrari F310   R
  E. Irvine   Ferrari F310   3
31 Mar   BRAZILIAN GP, Interlagos
  M. Schumacher   Ferrari F310   3
  E. Irvine   Ferrari F310   7
7 Apr   ARGENTINIAN GP, Buenos Aires
  M. Schumacher   Ferrari F310   R
  E. Irvine   Ferrari F310   5
28 Apr   EUROPEAN GP, Nürburgring
  M. Schumacher   Ferrari F310   2
  E. Irvine   Ferrari F310   R

5 May	SAN MARINO GP, Imola			27 Apr	SAN MARINO GP, Imola	
M. Schumacher	Ferrari F310	P/2		M. Schumacher	Ferrari F310B	2
E. Irvine	Ferrari F310	4		E. Irvine	Ferrari F310B	3

19 May	MONACO GP, Monte Carlo			11 May	MONACO GP, Monte Carlo	
M. Schumacher	Ferrari F310	P/R		M. Schumacher	Ferrari F310B	1/FL
E. Irvine	Ferrari F310	7/R		E. Irvine	Ferrari F310B	3

2 Jun	SPANISH GP, Montmelo			25 May	SPANISH GP, Montmelo	
M. Schumacher	Ferrari F310	1/FL		M. Schumacher	Ferrari F310B	4
E. Irvine	Ferrari F310	R		E. Irvine	Ferrari F310B	12

16 Jun	CANADIAN GP, Montreal			15 Jun	CANADIAN GP, Montreal	
M. Schumacher	Ferrari F310	R		M. Schumacher	Ferrari F310B	P/1
E. Irvine	Ferrari F310	R		E. Irvine	Ferrari F310B	R

30 Jun	FRENCH GP, Magny-Cours			29 Jun	FRENCH GP, Magny-Cours	
M. Schumacher	Ferrari F310	P/R		M. Schumacher	Ferrari F310B	P/1/FL
E. Irvine	Ferrari F310	R		E. Irvine	Ferrari F310B	3

14 Jul	BRITISH GP, Silverstone			13 Jul	BRITISH GP, Silverstone	
M. Schumacher	Ferrari F310	R		M. Schumacher	Ferrari F310B	R/FL
E. Irvine	Ferrari F310	R		E. Irvine	Ferrari F310B	R

28 Jul	GERMAN GP, Hockenheim			27 Jul	GERMAN GP, Hockenheim	
M. Schumacher	Ferrari F310	4		M. Schumacher	Ferrari F310B	2
E. Irvine	Ferrari F310	R		E. Irvine	Ferrari F310B	R

11 Aug	HUNGARIAN GP, Hungaroring			10 Aug	HUNGARIAN GP, Hungaroring	
M. Schumacher	Ferrari F310	P/9/R		M. Schumacher	Ferrari F310B	P/4
E. Irvine	Ferrari F310	R		E. Irvine	Ferrari F310B	9/R

25 Aug	BELGIAN GP, Spa-Francorchamps			24 Aug	BELGIAN GP, Spa-Francorchamps	
M. Schumacher	Ferrari F310	1		M. Schumacher	Ferrari F310B	1
E. Irvine	Ferrari F310	R		E. Irvine	Ferrari F310B	10/R

8 Sep	ITALIAN GP, Monza			7 Sep	ITALIAN GP, Monza	
M. Schumacher	Ferrari F310	1/FL		M. Schumacher	Ferrari F310B	6
E. Irvine	Ferrari F310	R		E. Irvine	Ferrari F310B	8

22 Sep	PORTUGUESE GP, Estoril			21 Sep	AUSTRIAN GP, A1-Ring	
M. Schumacher	Ferrari F310	3		M. Schumacher	Ferrari F310B	6
E. Irvine	Ferrari F310	5		E. Irvine	Ferrari F310B	R

13 Oct	JAPANESE GP, Suzuka			28 Sep	LUXEMBOURG GP, Nürburgring	
M. Schumacher	Ferrari F310	2		M. Schumacher	Ferrari F310B	R
E. Irvine	Ferrari F310	R		E. Irvine	Ferrari F310B	R

12 Oct	JAPANESE GP, Suzuka	
M. Schumacher	Ferrari F310B	1
E. Irvine	Ferrari F310B	3

1997

9 Mar	AUSTRALIAN GP, Melbourne	
M. Schumacher	Ferrari F310B	2
E. Irvine	Ferrari F310B	R

30 Mar	BRAZILIAN GP, Interlagos	
M. Schumacher	Ferrari F310B	5
E. Irvine	Ferrari F310B	16

13 Apr	ARGENTINIAN GP, Buenos Aires	
M. Schumacher	Ferrari F310B	R
E. Irvine	Ferrari F310B	2

26 Oct	EUROPEAN GP, Jerez de la Frontera	
M. Schumacher	Ferrari F310B	R
E. Irvine	Ferrari F310B	5

1998

8 Mar	AUSTRALIAN GP, Melbourne	
M. Schumacher	Ferrari F300	R
E. Irvine	Ferrari F300	4

29 Mar BRAZILIAN GP, Interlagos
  M. Schumacher   Ferrari F300   3
  E. Irvine   Ferrari F300   8
12 Apr ARGENTINIAN GP, Buenos Aires
  M. Schumacher   Ferrari F300   1
  E. Irvine   Ferrari F300   3
26 Apr SAN MARINO GP, Imola
  M. Schumacher   Ferrari F300   2/FL
  E. Irvine   Ferrari F300   3
10 May SPANISH GP, Montmelo
  M. Schumacher   Ferrari F300   3
  E. Irvine   Ferrari F300   R
24 May MONACO GP, Monte Carlo
  M. Schumacher   Ferrari F300   10
  E. Irvine   Ferrari F300   3
7 Jun CANADIAN GP, Montreal
  M. Schumacher   Ferrari F300   1/FL
  E. Irvine   Ferrari F300   3
28 Jun FRENCH GP, Magny-Cours
  M. Schumacher   Ferrari F300   1
  E. Irvine   Ferrari F300   2
12 Jul BRITISH GP, Silverstone
  M. Schumacher   Ferrari F300   1/FL
  E. Irvine   Ferrari F300   3
26 Jul AUSTRIAN GP, A1-Ring
  M. Schumacher   Ferrari F300   3
  E. Irvine   Ferrari F300   4
2 Aug GERMAN GP, Hockenheim
  M. Schumacher   Ferrari F300   5
  E. Irvine   Ferrari F300   8
16 Aug HUNGARIAN GP, Hungaroring
  M. Schumacher   Ferrari F300   1/FL
  E. Irvine   Ferrari F300   R
30 Aug BELGIAN GP, Spa-Francorchamps
  M. Schumacher   Ferrari F300   R/FL
  E. Irvine   Ferrari F300   R
13 Sep ITALIAN GP, Monza
  M. Schumacher   Ferrari F300   P/1
  E. Irvine   Ferrari F300   2
27 Sep LUXEMBOURG GP, Nürburgring
  M. Schumacher   Ferrari F300   P/2
  E. Irvine   Ferrari F300   4
1 Nov JAPANESE GP, Suzuka
  M. Schumacher   Ferrari F300   P/R/FL
  E. Irvine   Ferrari F300   2

1999

7 Mar AUSTRALIAN GP, Melbourne
  M. Schumacher   Ferrari F399   8/FL
  E. Irvine   Ferrari F399   1
11 Apr BRAZILIAN GP, Interlagos
  M. Schumacher   Ferrari F399   2
  E. Irvine   Ferrari F399   5
30 Apr SAN MARINO GP, Imola
  M. Schumacher   Ferrari F399   1/FL
  E. Irvine   Ferrari F399   R
16 May MONACO GP, Monte Carlo
  M. Schumacher   Ferrari F399   1
  E. Irvine   Ferrari F399   2
30 May SPANISH GP, Montmelo
  M. Schumacher   Ferrari F399   3/FL
  E. Irvine   Ferrari F399   4
13 Jun CANADIAN GP, Montreal
  M. Schumacher   Ferrari F399   P/R/FL
  E. Irvine   Ferrari F399   3/FL
27 Jun FRENCH GP, Magny-Cours
  M. Schumacher   Ferrari F399   5
  E. Irvine   Ferrari F399   6
11 Jul BRITISH GP, Silverstone
  M. Schumacher   Ferrari F399   R
  E. Irvine   Ferrari F399   2
25 Jul AUSTRIAN GP, A1-Ring
  M. Salo   Ferrari F399   9
  E. Irvine   Ferrari F399   1
1 Aug GERMAN GP, Hockenheim
  M. Salo   Ferrari F399   2
  E. Irvine   Ferrari F399   1
15 Aug HUNGARIAN GP, Hungaroring
  M. Salo   Ferrari F399   12
  E. Irvine   Ferrari F399   3
29 Aug BELGIAN GP, Spa-Francorchamps
  M. Salo   Ferrari F399   7
  E. Irvine   Ferrari F399   4
12 Sep ITALIAN GP, Monza
  M. Salo   Ferrari F399   3
  E. Irvine   Ferrari F399   6
26 Sep EUROPEAN GP, Nürburgring
  M. Salo   Ferrari F399   R
  E. Irvine   Ferrari F399   7
17 Oct MALAYSIAN GP, Sepang
  M. Schumacher   Ferrari F399   P/2/FL
  E. Irvine   Ferrari F399   1

31 Oct   JAPANESE GP, Suzuka
M. Schumacher   Ferrari F399   P/2/FL
E. Irvine   Ferrari F399   3

2000

12 Mar   AUSTRALIAN GP, Melbourne
M. Schumacher   Ferrari F1-2000   1
R. Barrichello   Ferrari F1-2000   2/FL
26 Mar   BRAZILIAN GP, Interlagos
M. Schumacher   Ferrari F1-2000   1/FL
R. Barrichello   Ferrari F1-2000   R
9 Apr   SAN MARINO GP, Imola
M. Schumacher   Ferrari F1-2000   1
R. Barrichello   Ferrari F1-2000   4
23 Apr   BRITISH GP, Silverstone
M. Schumacher   Ferrari F1-2000   3
R. Barrichello   Ferrari F1-2000   P/R
7 May   SPANISH GP, Montmelo
M. Schumacher   Ferrari F1-2000   P/5
R. Barrichello   Ferrari F1-2000   3
21 May   EUROPEAN GP, Nürburgring
M. Schumacher   Ferrari F1-2000   1/FL
R. Barrichello   Ferrari F1-2000   4
4 Jun   MONACO GP, Monte Carlo
M. Schumacher   Ferrari F1-2000   P/R
R. Barrichello   Ferrari F1-2000   2

18 Jun   CANADIAN GP, Montreal
M. Schumacher   Ferrari F1-2000   P/1
R. Barrichello   Ferrari F1-2000   2
2 Jul   FRENCH GP, Magny-Cours
M. Schumacher   Ferrari F1-2000   P/R
R. Barrichello   Ferrari F1-2000   3
16 Jul   AUSTRIAN GP, A1-Ring
M. Schumacher   Ferrari F1-2000   R
R. Barrichello   Ferrari F1-2000   3
30 Jul   GERMAN GP, Hockenheim
M. Schumacher   Ferrari F1-2000   R
R. Barrichello   Ferrari F1-2000   1/FL
13 Aug   HUNGARIAN GP, Hungaroring
M. Schumacher   Ferrari F1-2000   P/2
R. Barrichello   Ferrari F1-2000   4
27 Aug   BELGIAN GP, Spa-Francorchamps
M. Schumacher   Ferrari F1-2000   2
R. Barrichello   Ferrari F1-2000   R/FL
10 Sep   ITALIAN GP, Monza
M. Schumacher   Ferrari F1-2000   P/1
R. Barrichello   Ferrari F1-2000   R
24 Sep   USA GP, Indianapolis
M. Schumacher   Ferrari F1-2000   P/1
R. Barrichello   Ferrari F1-2000   2
8 Oct   JAPANESE GP, Suzuka
M. Schumacher   Ferrari F1-2000   P/1
R. Barrichello   Ferrari F1-2000   4
22 Oct   MALAYSIAN GP, Sepang
M. Schumacher   Ferrari F1-2000   P/1
R. Barrichello   Ferrari F1-2000   3

Appendix 2

Ferrari –
team statistics

F1 WORLD CHAMPIONSHIP RECORD
TO END OF 2000:

Grands Prix contested: 663
Pole positions: 137
Victories: 135
Fastest race laps: 144
Points: 2,528.5
World Championships for Drivers: 10
World Championships for Constructors: 10
(*All outright records*)

CONSTRUCTORS'
CHAMPIONSHIP PLACINGS:

1958	–	2nd	40 (17) points
1959	–	2nd	32 (6) points
1960	–	3rd	26 (1) points
1961	–	1st	40 (12) points
1962	–	5th=	18 points
1963	–	4th	26 points
1964	–	1st	45 (4) points
1965	–	4th	26 (1) points
1966	–	2nd	31 (1) points
1967	–	4th=	20 points
1968	–	4th	32 points
1969	–	5th=	7 points
1970	–	2nd	52 (3) points
1971	–	3rd=	33 points
1972	–	4th	33 points
1973	–	6th=	12 points
1974	–	2nd	65 points
1975	–	1st	72.5 points
1976	–	1st	83 points
1977	–	1st	95 (2) points
1978	–	2nd	58 points
1979	–	1st	113 points
1980	–	10th	8 points
1981	–	5th	34 points
1982	–	1st	74 points
1983	–	1st	89 points
1984	–	2nd	57.5 points
1985	–	2nd	82 points
1986	–	4th	37 points
1987	–	4th	53 points
1988	–	2nd	65 points
1989	–	3rd	59 points
1990	–	2nd	110 points
1991	–	3rd	55.5 points
1992	–	4th	21 points
1993	–	4th	28 points
1994	–	3rd	71 points
1995	–	3rd	73 points
1996	–	2nd	70 points
1997	–	2nd	102 points
1998	–	2nd	133 points
1999	–	1st	128 points
2000	–	1st	170 points

Bracketed figure denotes points scored but
not counted towards Championship total.

189

Appendix

Ferrari – most successful drivers

MICHAEL SCHUMACHER (D). Born 3.1.69. F1 debut, 1991, Belgium (Jordan). Has driven for Ferrari from 1996. 44 career wins, 25 with Ferrari. World Champion, 1994 and '95 (Benetton), 2000 (Ferrari).

NIKI LAUDA (A). Born 22.2.49. F1 debut, 1971, Austria (March). Drove for Ferrari 1974–77. 25 career wins, 15 with Ferrari. World Champion, 1975 and '77 (Ferrari) and '84 (McLaren).

ALBERTO ASCARI (I). Born 13.7.18. Died 26.5.55. F1 debut, 1950, Monaco (Ferrari). Drove for Ferrari 1950–53 and 1 race in '54. 13 career wins, all with Ferrari. World Champion, 1952 and '53 (Ferrari).

JACKY ICKX (B). Born 1.1.45. F1 debut, 1966, Germany (Matra). Drove for Ferrari 1968 and 1970–73. 8 career wins, 6 with Ferrari.

GILLES VILLENEUVE (CDN). Born 18.1.50. Died 8.5.82. F1 debut, 1977, Britain (McLaren). Drove for Ferrari 1977–82. 6 career wins, all with Ferrari.

GERHARD BERGER (A). Born 27.8.59. F1 debut, 1984, Austria (ATS). Drove for Ferrari 1987–89 and 1993–95. 10 career wins, 5 with Ferrari.

ALAIN PROST (F). Born 24.2.55. F1 debut, 1980, Argentina (McLaren). Drove for Ferrari 1990–91. 51 career wins, 5 with Ferrari. World Champion, 1985, '86 and '89 (McLaren) and 1993 (Williams).

CARLOS REUTEMANN (RA). Born 12.4.42. F1 debut, 1972, Argentina (Brabham). Drove for Ferrari end of 1976–78. 12 career wins, 5 with Ferrari.

EDDIE IRVINE (GB). Born 10.11.65. F1 debut, 1993, Japan (Jordan). Drove for Ferrari 1996–99. 4 career wins, all with Ferrari.

CLAY REGAZZONI (I). Born 5.9.39. F1 debut, 1970, Netherlands (Ferrari). Drove for Ferrari 1970–72 and '74–76. 5 career wins, 4 with Ferrari.

JOHN SURTEES (GB). Born 11.2.34. F1 debut, 1960, Monaco (Lotus). Drove for Ferrari 1963–66. 6 career wins, 4 with Ferrari. World Champion, 1964 (Ferrari).

PETER COLLINS (GB). Born 6.11.31. Died 3.8.58. F1 debut, 1952, Switzerland (HWM). Drove for Ferrari 1956–58. 3 career wins, all with Ferrari.

JUAN MANUEL FANGIO (RA). Born 24.6.11. Died 17.7.95. F1 debut, 1948, France (Simca Gordini). Drove for Ferrari, 1956. 24 career wins, 3 with Ferrari. World Champion, 1951 (Alfa Romeo), '54 (Maserati and Mercedes), '55 (Mercedes), '56 (Ferrari) and '57 (Maserati).

MIKE HAWTHORN (GB). Born 10.4.29. Died 22.1.59. F1 debut, 1952, Belgium (Cooper). Drove for Ferrari, 1953–55 and 1957–58. 3 career wins, all with Ferrari. World Champion, 1958 (Ferrari).

PHIL HILL (USA). Born 20.4.27. F1 debut, 1958, France (Maserati). Drove for Ferrari, 1958–62. 3 career wins, all with Ferrari. World Champion, 1961 (Ferrari).

NIGEL MANSELL (GB). Born 8.8.53. F1 debut, 1980, Austria (Lotus). Drove for Ferrari, 1989–90. 31 career wins, 3 with Ferrari. World Champion, 1992 (Williams).

JODY SCHECKTER (ZA). Born 29.1.50. F1 debut, 1972, USA (McLaren). Drove for Ferrari, 1979–80. 10 career wins, 3 with Ferrari. World Champion, 1979 (Ferrari).

Other Ferrari winning drivers:

3 wins – Michele Alboreto; René Arnoux.

2 wins – Tony Brooks; Froilan Gonzalez; Didier Pironi; Patrick Tambay; Wolfgang von Trips.

1 win – Jean Alesi; Mario Andretti; Giancarlo Baghetti; Lorenzo Bandini; Rubens Barrichello; Giuseppe Farina; Luigi Musso; Ludovico Scarfiotti; Piero Taruffi; Maurice Trintignant.

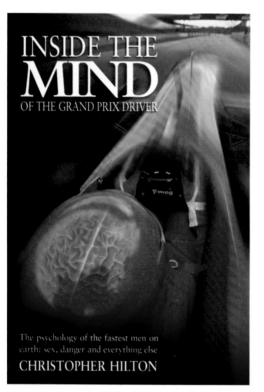
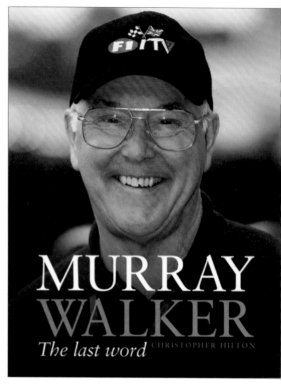